BIG-NOTE PIANO

CHART HITS OF 2020

ISBN 978-1-5400-8512-2

Visit Hal Leonard Online at
www.halleonard.com

Contact us:
Hal Leonard
7777 West Bluemound Road
Milwaukee, WI 53213
Email: info@halleonard.com

In Europe, contact:
Hal Leonard Europe Limited
42 Wigmore Street
Marylebone, London, W1U 2RN
Email: info@halleonardeurope.com

In Australia, contact:
Hal Leonard Australia Pty. Ltd.
4 Lentara Court
Cheltenham, Victoria, 3192 Australia
Email: info@halleonard.com.au

BEAUTIFUL PEOPLE

Words and Music by ED SHEERAN,
KHALID ROBINSON, FRED GIBSON,
MAX MARTIN and SHELLBACK

Moderate R&B groove

5
town. Ev - 'ry - bod - y's look-ing for a come-up,
and they want to know what you're a -

3
bout. Me in the mid-dle with the one I love and
we're just try'n' to fig - ure ev - 'ry - thing

out. We don't fit in well
'cause we are just our-selves.
I could use some help

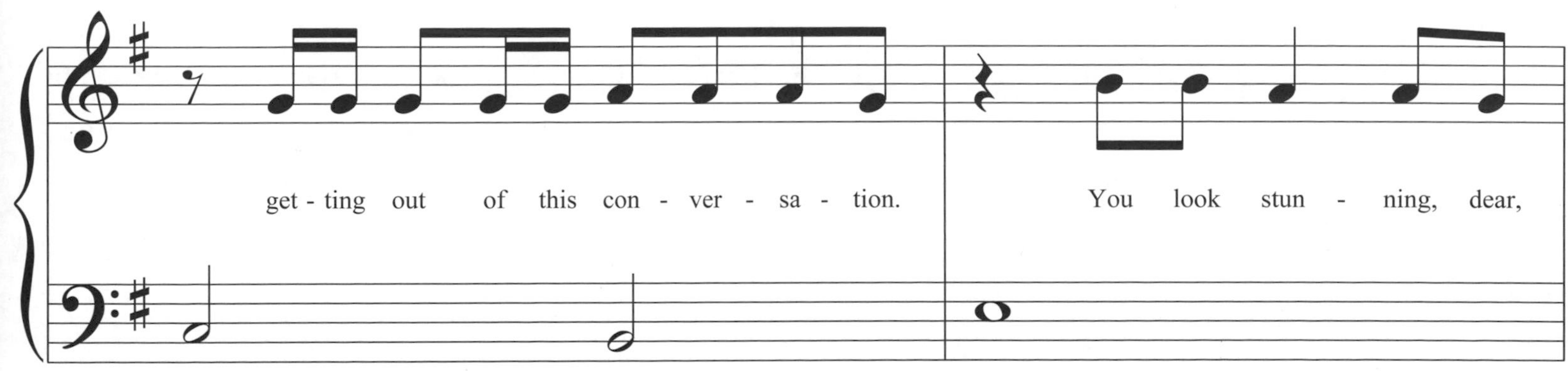
get - ting out of this con - ver - sa - tion.
You look stun - ning, dear,

3
so don't ask that ques - tion here.
This is my on - ly fear,

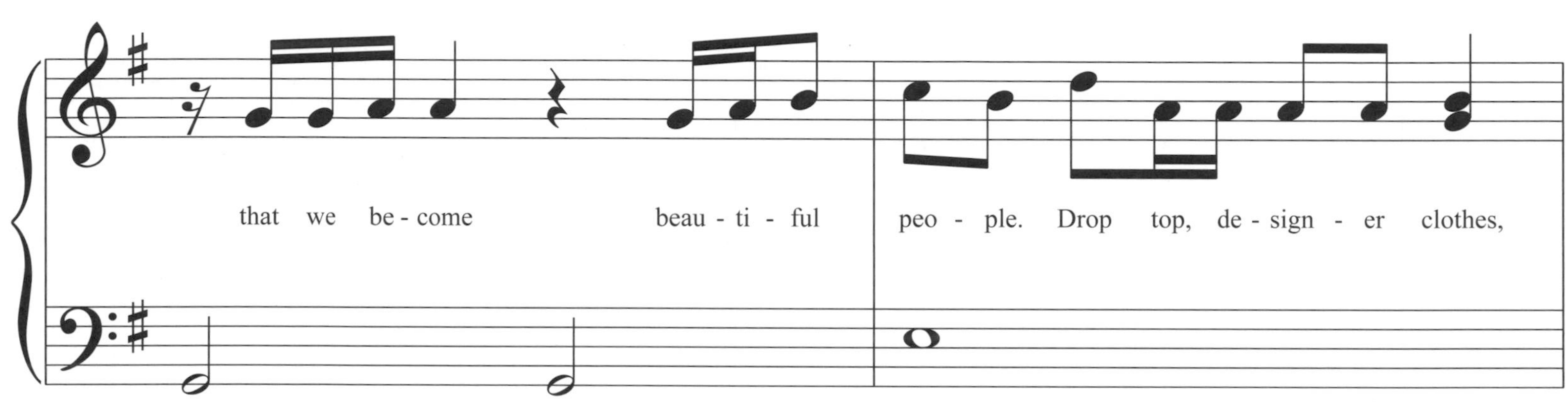
that we be - come beau - ti - ful
peo - ple. Drop top, de - sign - er clothes,

front row at fash - ion shows.
"What d'you do and who d'you know?"

In - side the world of beau - ti - ful
peo - ple. Cham - pagne and rolled - up notes,

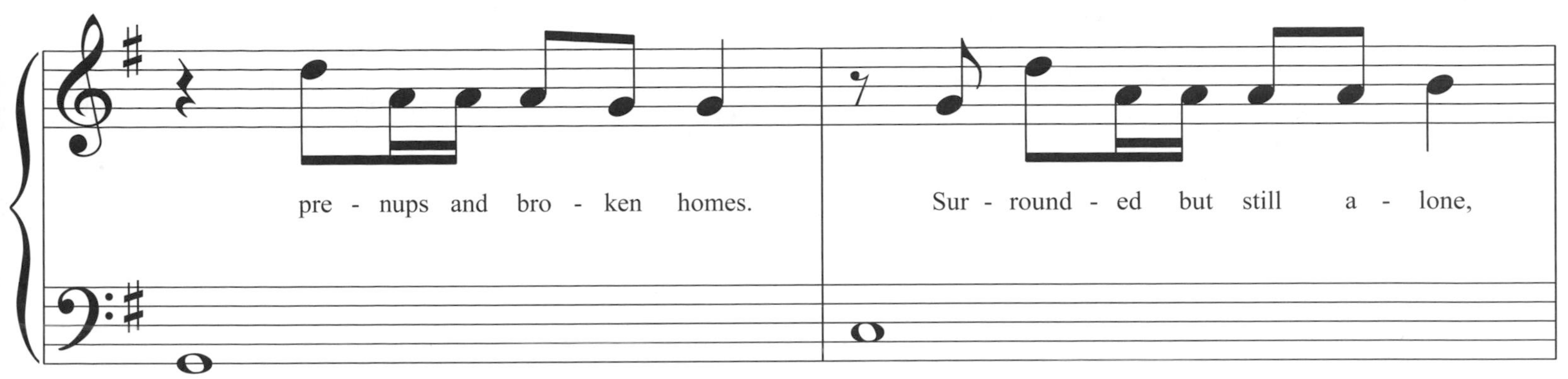
pre - nups and bro - ken homes.
Sur - round - ed but still a - lone,

let's leave the par - ty. That's not
who we are.
(We

5
are, we are, we are.) We are not
beau - ti - ful.

1
Yeah, that's not
who we are.
(We

5
To Coda
are, we are, we are.) We are not
beau - ti - ful.
L.

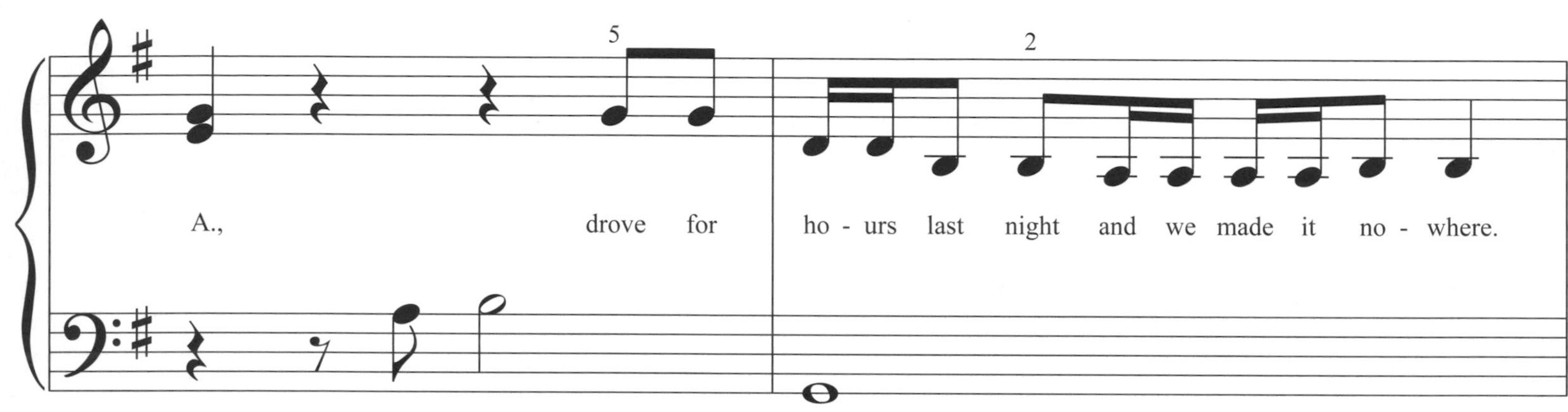
5
2
A., drove for
ho - urs last night and we made it no - where.

I see stars
in your eyes when we're half - way there.

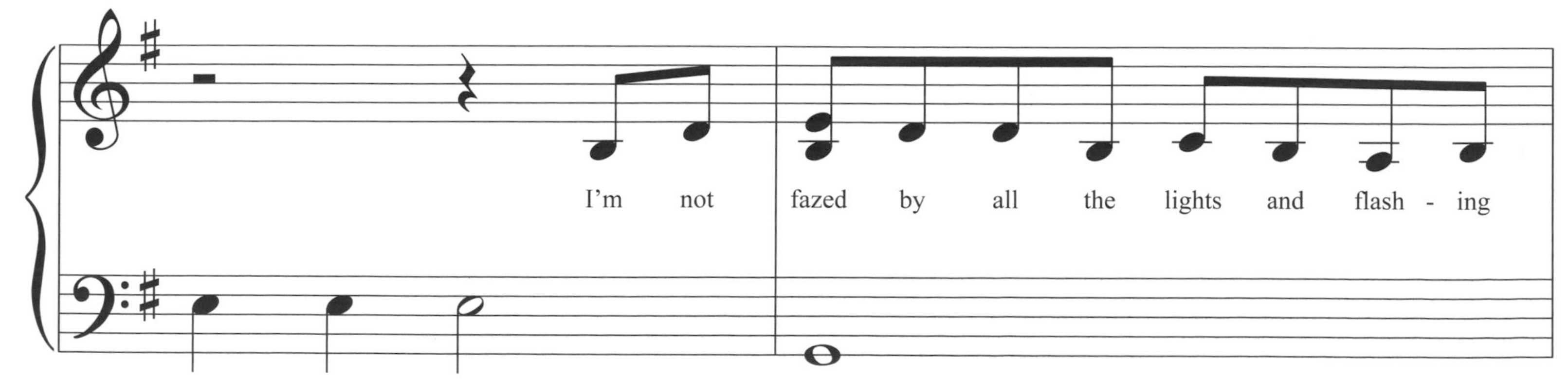
I'm not
fazed by all the lights and flash - ing

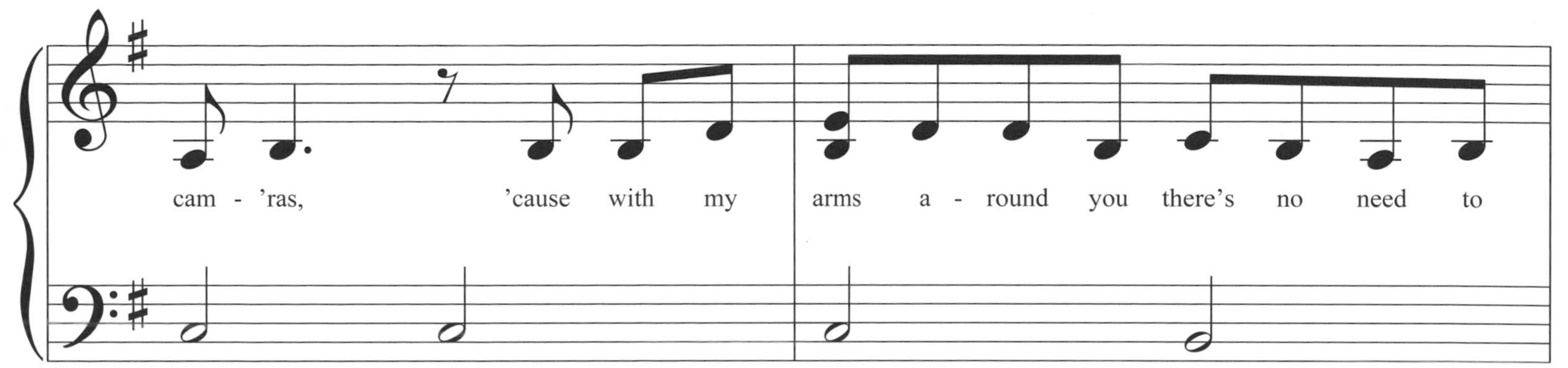
cam - 'ras, 'cause with my
arms a - round you there's no need to

D.S. al Coda
care. We don't fit in well

CODA

3
(We
are, we are, we are.) We are not

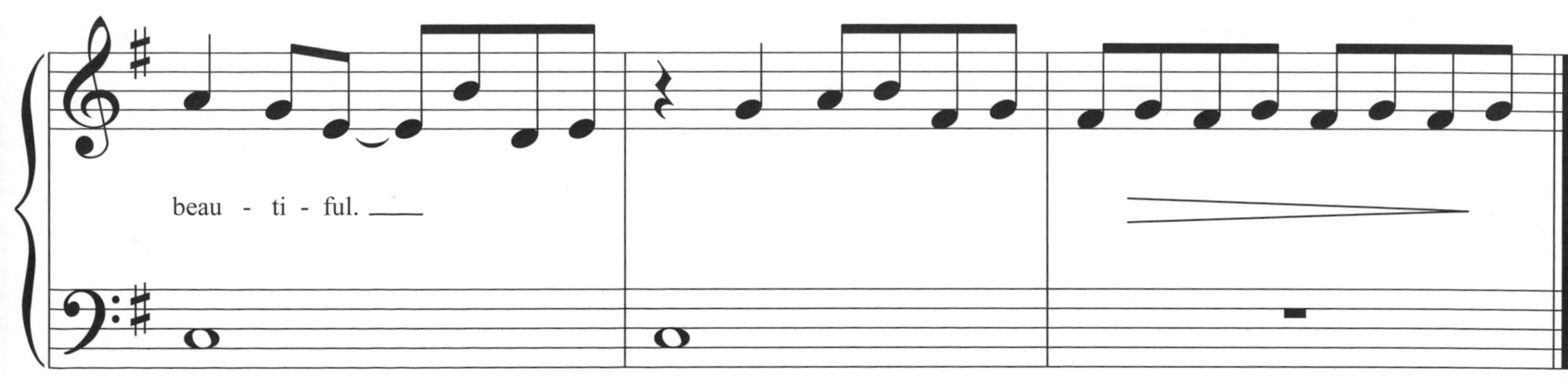
beau - ti - ful.

DANCE MONKEY

Words and Music by
TONI WATSON

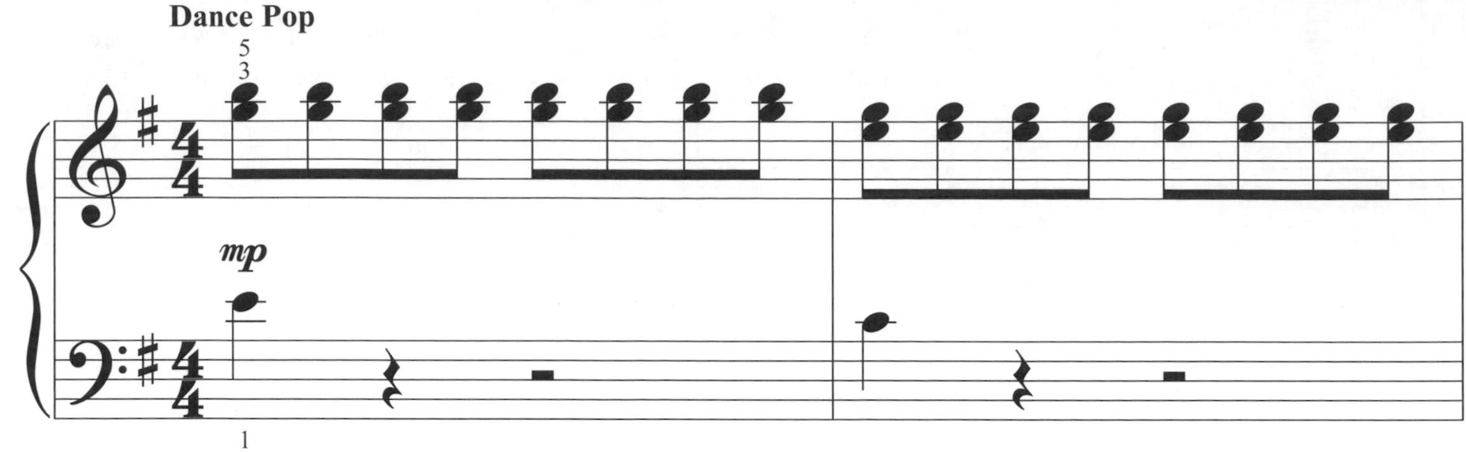

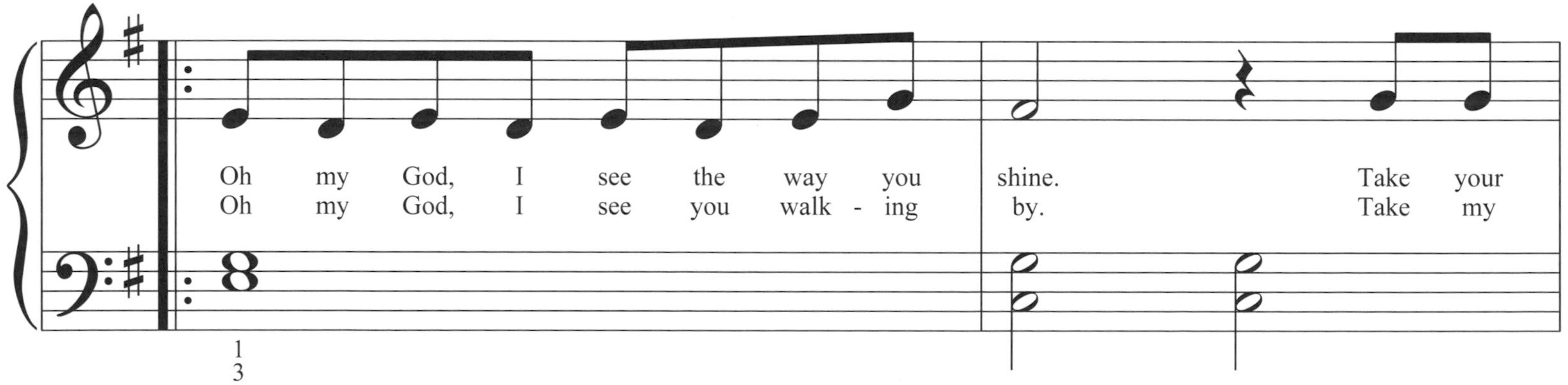

stopped me dead while I was pass - ing by. And now I
mon - key, I've been danc - ing my whole life. But you just

beg to see you dance just one more time.
beg to see me dance just one more time.
Ooh, I

see you, see you, see you ev - 'ry time, and oh, my,

I, I, I, I like your style. You, you make me, make me, make me want to

cry, and now I beg to see you dance just one more time. So they say:

Dance for me, dance for me, dance for me, oh, oh. I've nev - er
2

seen an - y - bod - y do the things you do be - fore. They say:

Move for me, move for me, move for me, ay, ay. And when you're

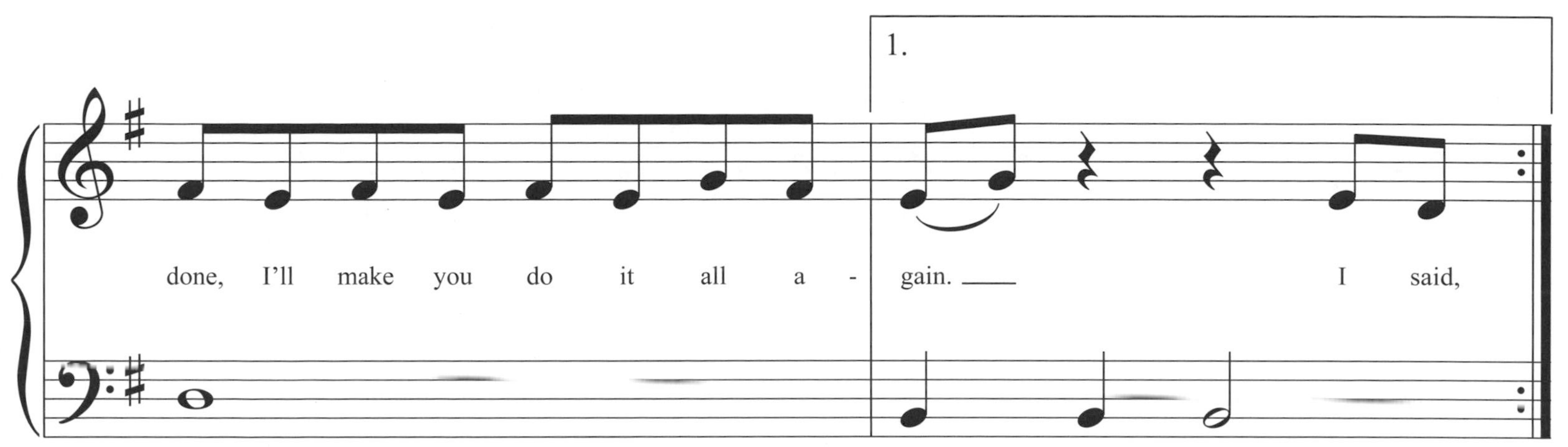
1.
done, I'll make you do it all a - gain. ___ I said,

2.
gain. ___ They say: Dance for me, dance for me, dance for me, oh,

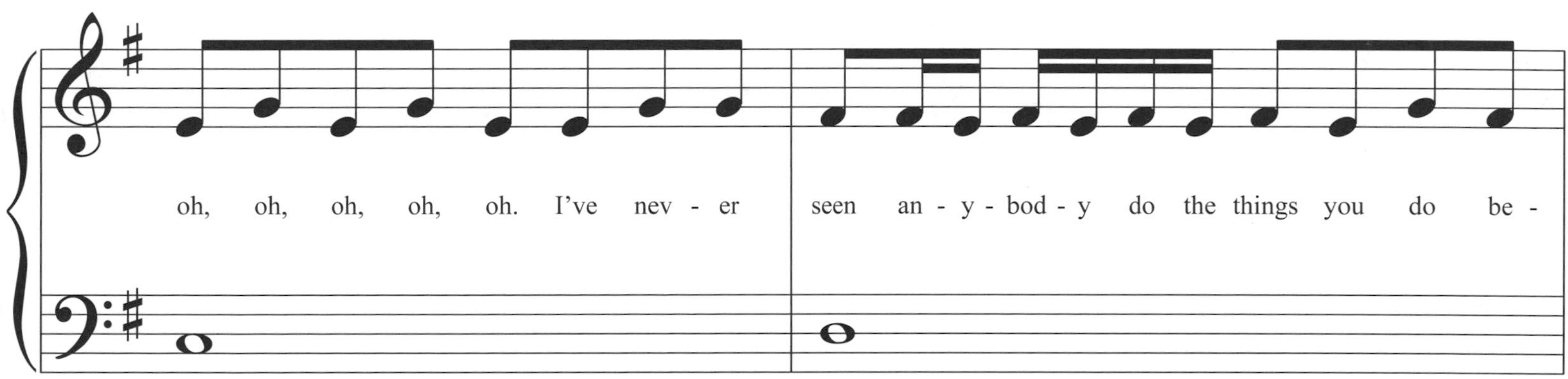
oh, oh, oh, oh, oh. I've nev - er seen an - y - bod - y do the things you do be -

fore. ___ They say: Move for me, move for me, move for me, ay,

ay. And when you're done, I'll make you do it all a - gain.

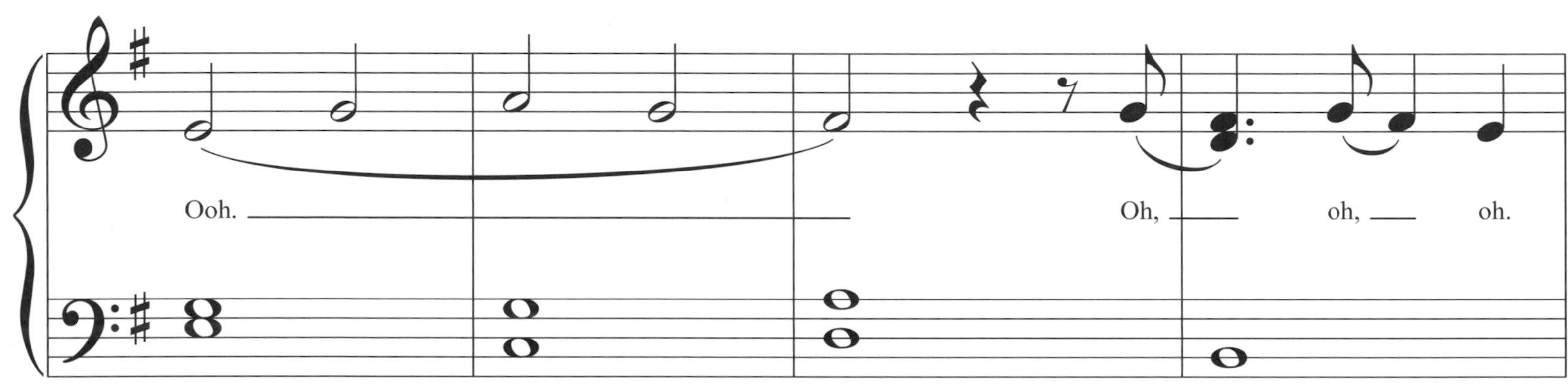
Ooh.
Oh, oh, oh.

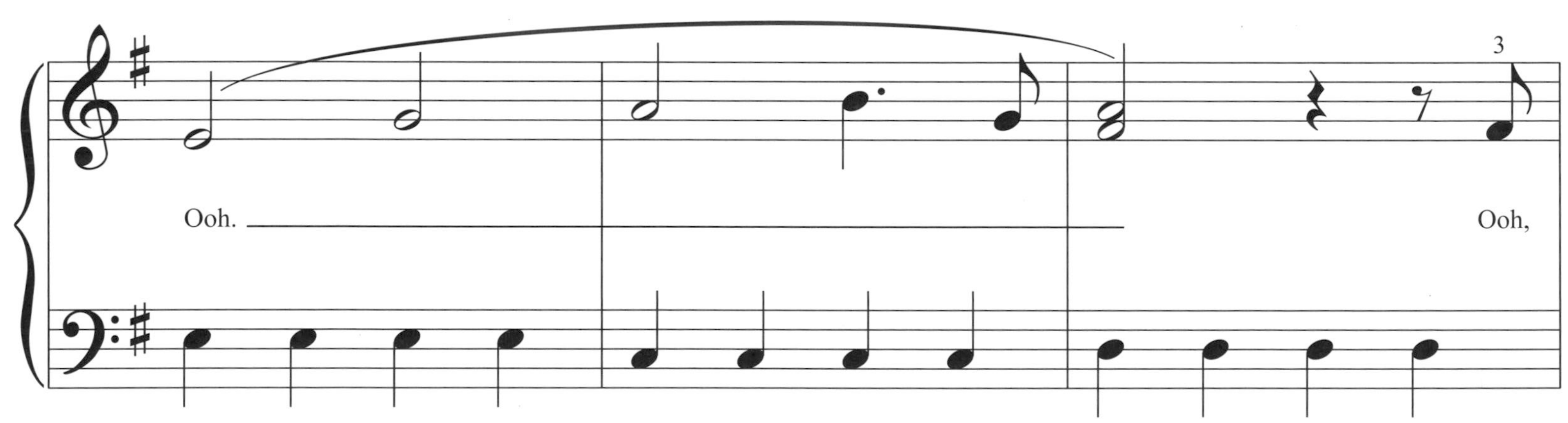
3
Ooh.
Ooh,

oh, oh. They say: Dance for me, dance for me, dance for me, oh,

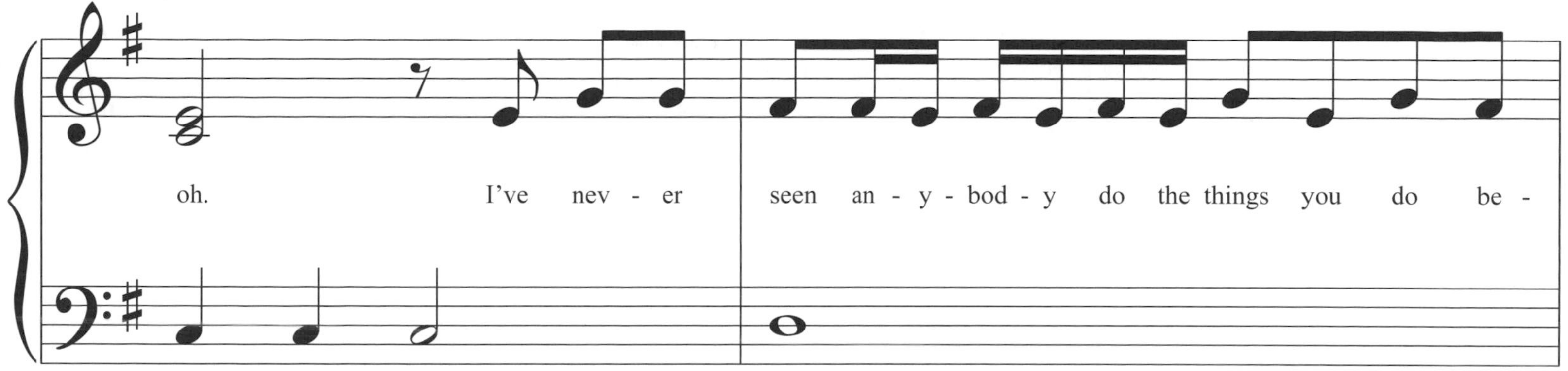
oh. I've nev - er
seen an - y - bod - y do the things you do be -

fore. They say:
Move for me, move for me, move for me, ay,

ay. And when you're
done, I'll make you do it all a -

gain. They say:
Dance for me, dance for me, dance for me, oh,

oh, oh, oh, oh, oh. I've nev - er
seen an - y - bod - y do the things you do be -

fore. ___ They say:
Move for me, move for me, move for me, ay,

ay. And when you're
done, I'll make you do it all a -

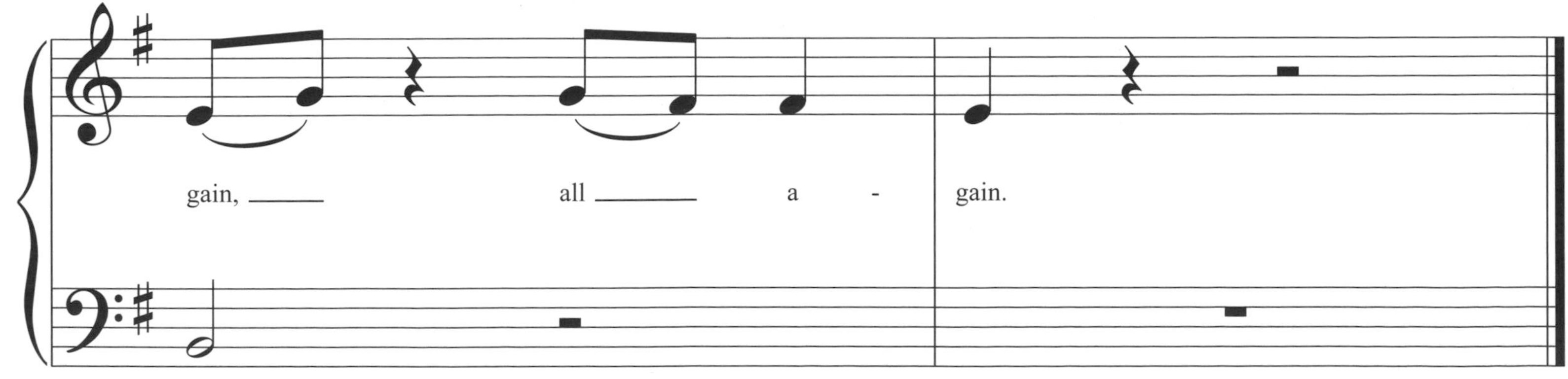
gain, ___ all ___ a - gain.

BLINDING LIGHTS

Words and Music by ABEL TESFAYE,
MAX MARTIN, JASON QUENNEVILLE,
OSCAR HOLTER and AHMAD BALSHE

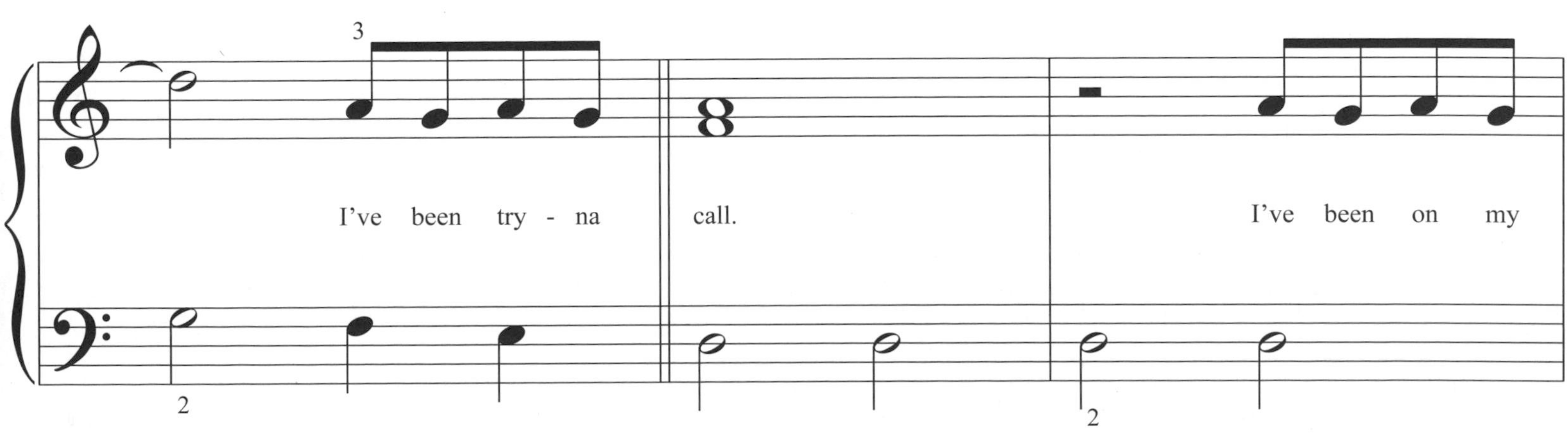

own for long e - nough. May - be you can show me how to

4
2
love, may - be.
I'm go - in' through with -
2

drawls. You don't e - ven have to do too
time, 'cause I can see the sun light up the
2

4
much. You can turn me on with just a touch, ba -
sky. So I hit the road in o - ver - drive, ba -

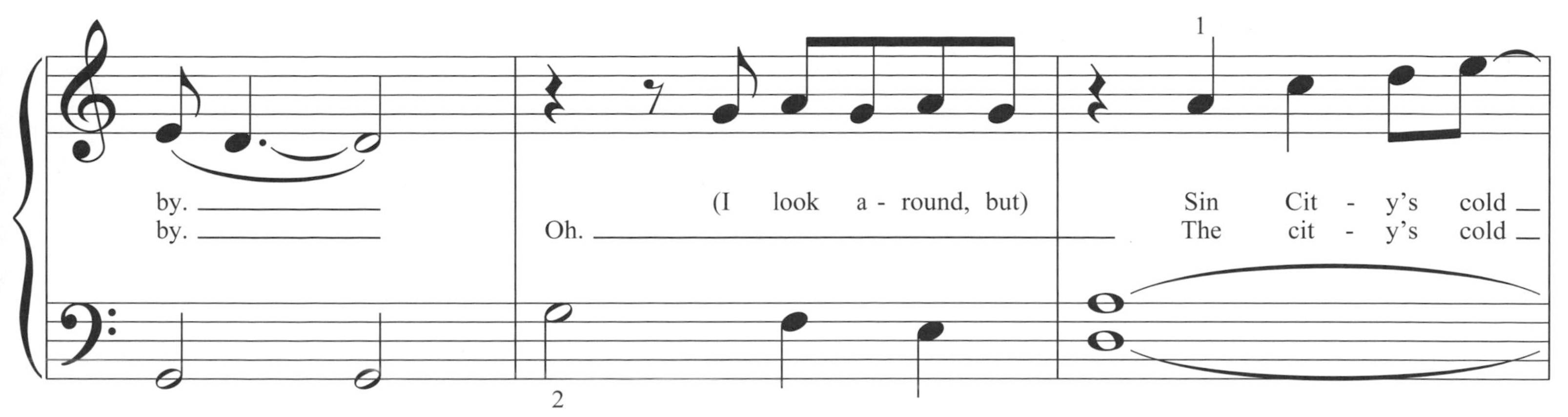
1
by.
by.
(I look a - round, but)
Oh.
Sin Cit - y's cold
The cit - y's cold
2

and emp - ty.
and emp - ty.
No one's a - round to judge me.

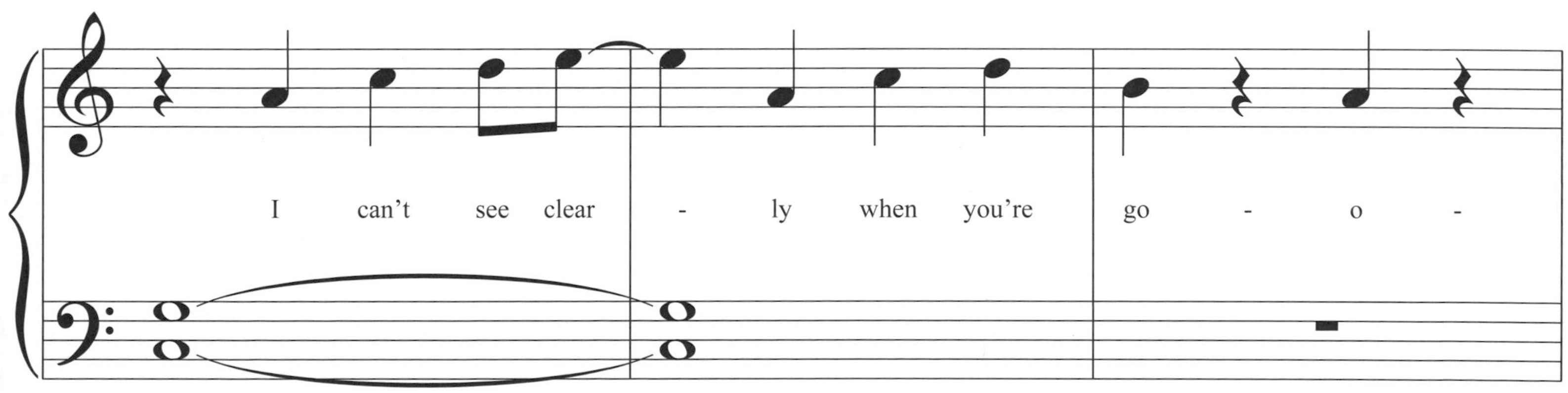
I can't see clear - ly when you're go - o -

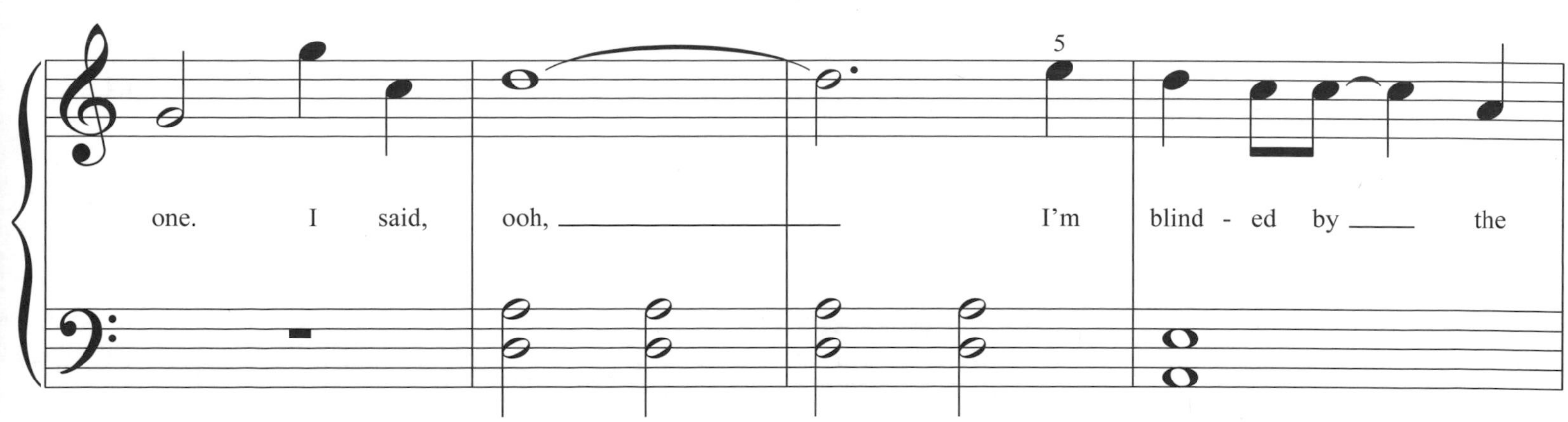
5
one. I said, ooh, I'm blind - ed by the

1
lights. No, I can't sleep un - til I feel your touch.

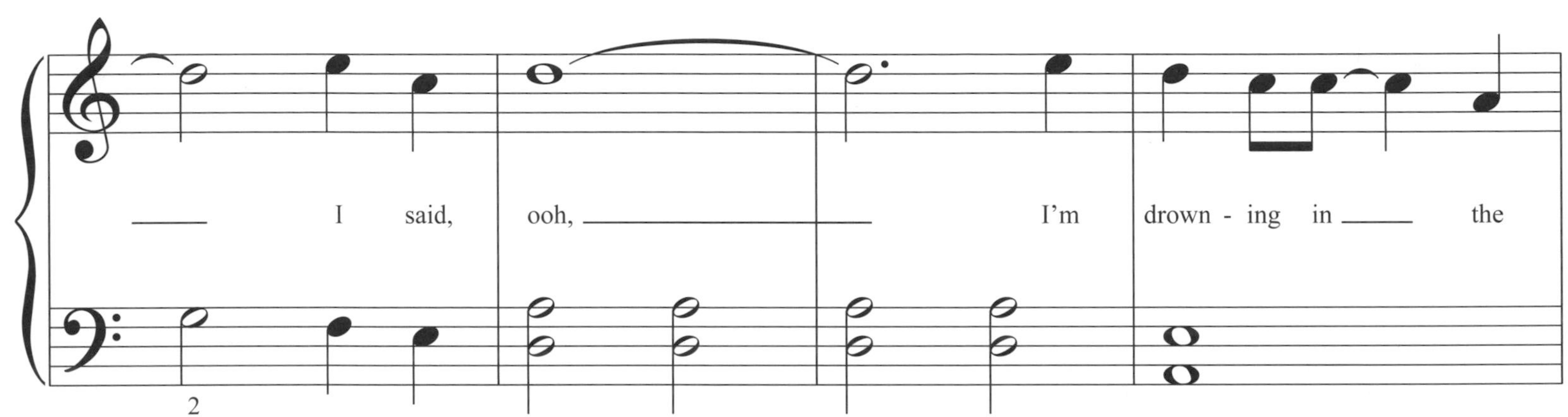
I said, ooh, I'm drown - ing in the
2

To Coda
1
night. Oh, when I'm like this, you're the one I

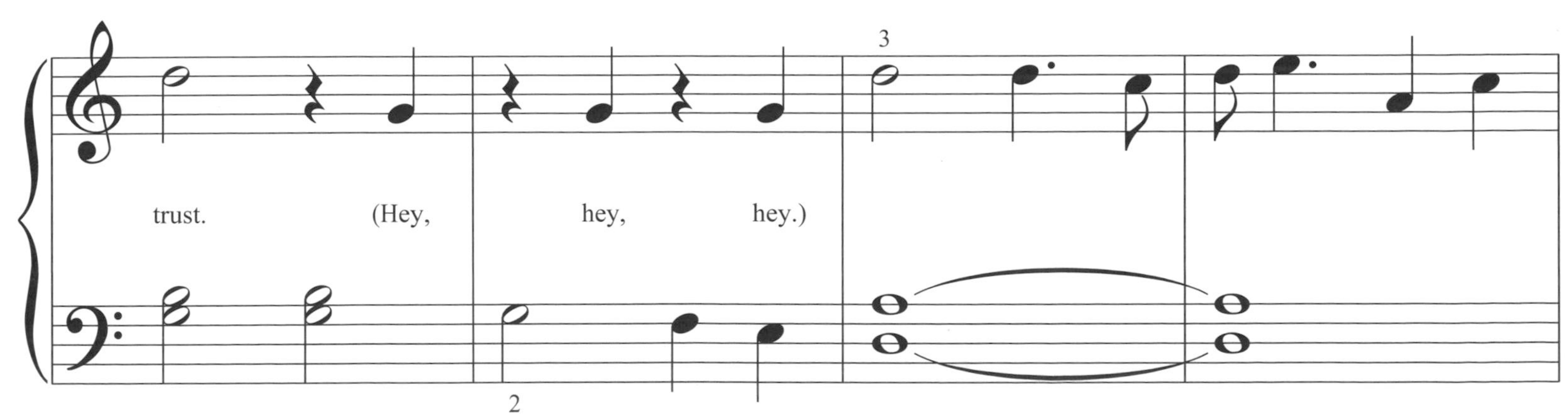
3
trust. (Hey, hey, hey.)
2

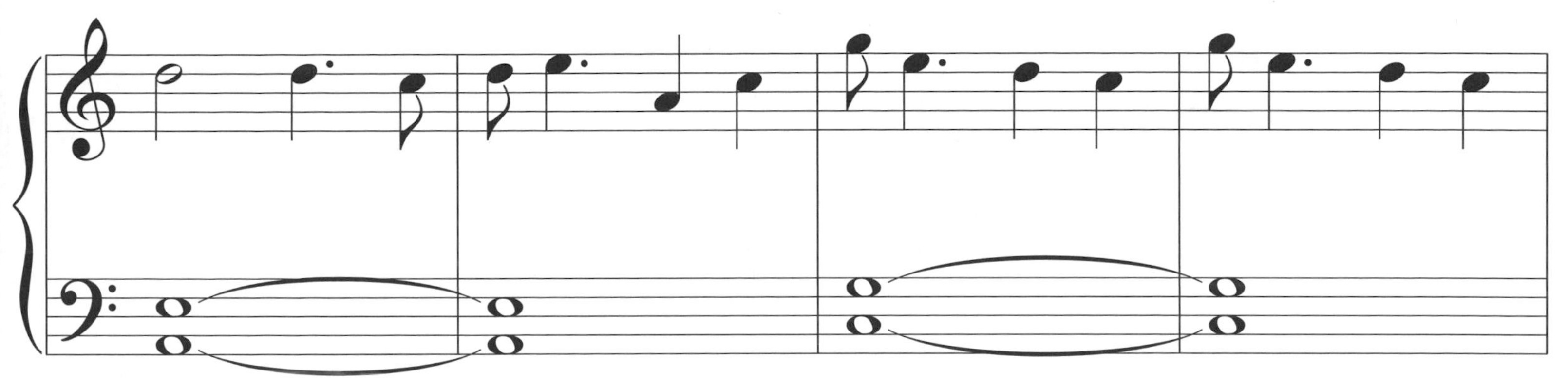

D.S. al Coda
2
I'm run-ning out of
2

CODA
you're the one I

4
trust.
I'm just walk - in' by to let you
2

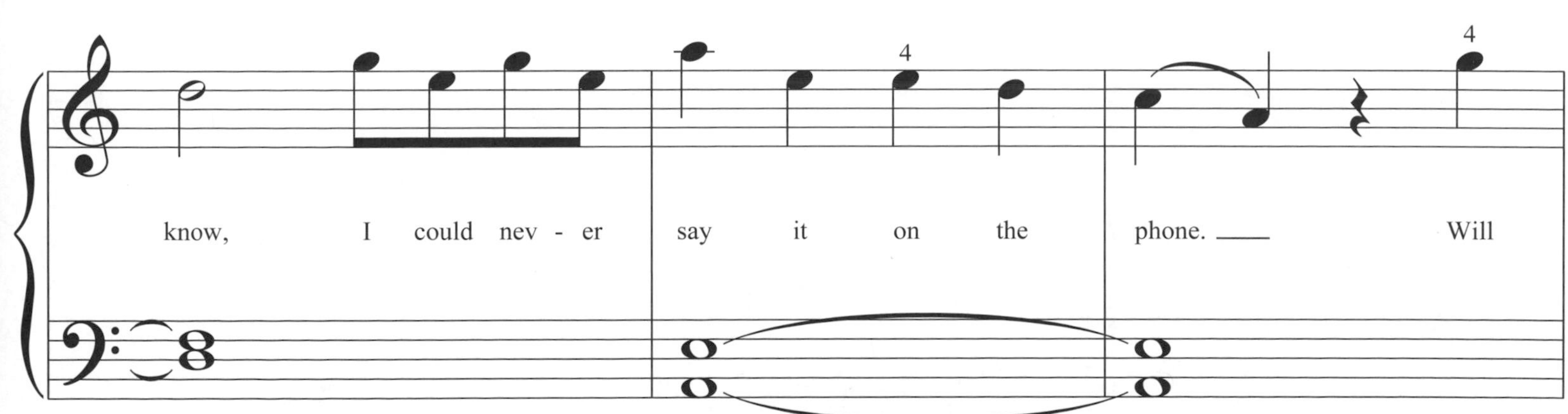
4
4
know, I could nev - er say it on the phone. ___ Will

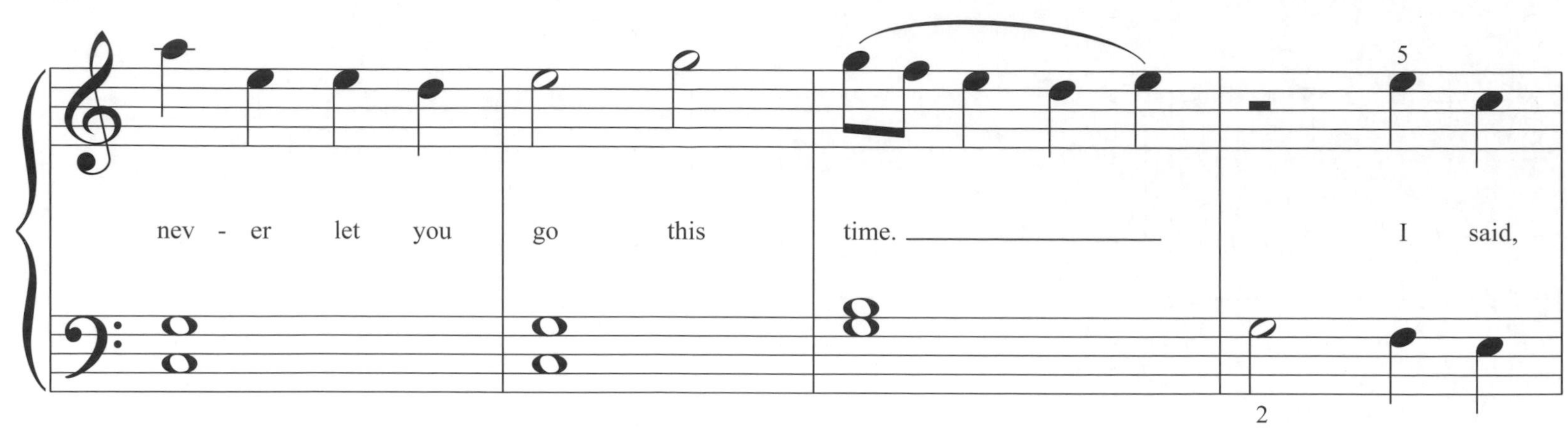
5
nev - er let you go this time. I said,
2

ooh, I'm blind - ed by the lights.

1
No, I can't sleep un - til I feel your touch. (Hey,

3
hey, hey.)

1.
(Hey,
2.
hey.)
I said, ooh,
I'm blind - ed by the lights.
No,
I can't sleep un - til I feel your touch.

DON'T START NOW

Words and Music by DUA LIPA,
CAROLINE AILIN, IAN KIRKPATRICK
and EMILY SCHWARTZ

good al - read - y, so moved on, it's scar - y. I'm not where you left ___ me at all. _

___ So, ___ if you don't want to see me danc - ing with some -

4
2
bod - y, if you want to be -

2
lieve that an - y - thing could stop me: Don't show

up, don't come out, don't start car - ing a - bout me now. Walk a -
way; you know how. Don't start car - ing a - bout me now. Aren't you the
1.
2.
now. (Up, up, don't come out.
Don't show up, up, up. Don't start now. Up, up,

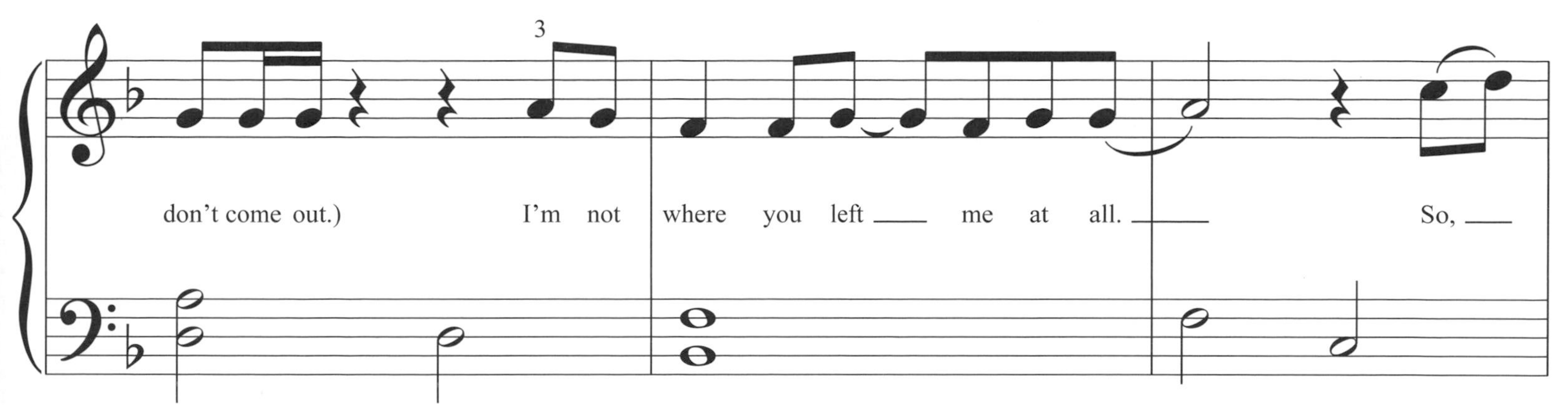
3
don't come out.) I'm not where you left me at all. So,

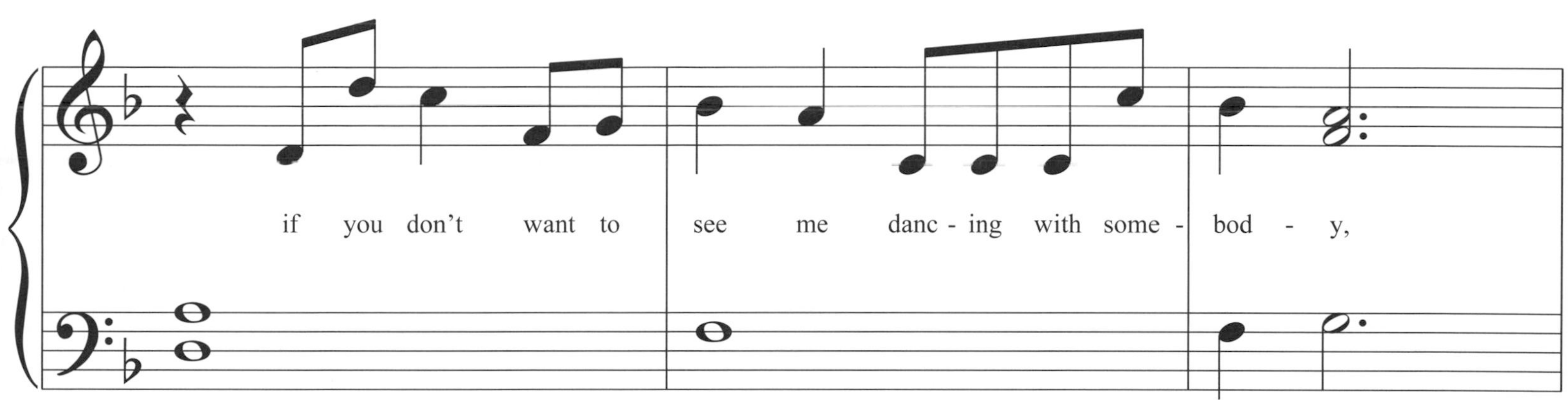
if you don't want to see me danc - ing with some - bod - y,

4
2
if you want to be - lieve that an - y - thing could

2
stop me: Don't show up, don't come

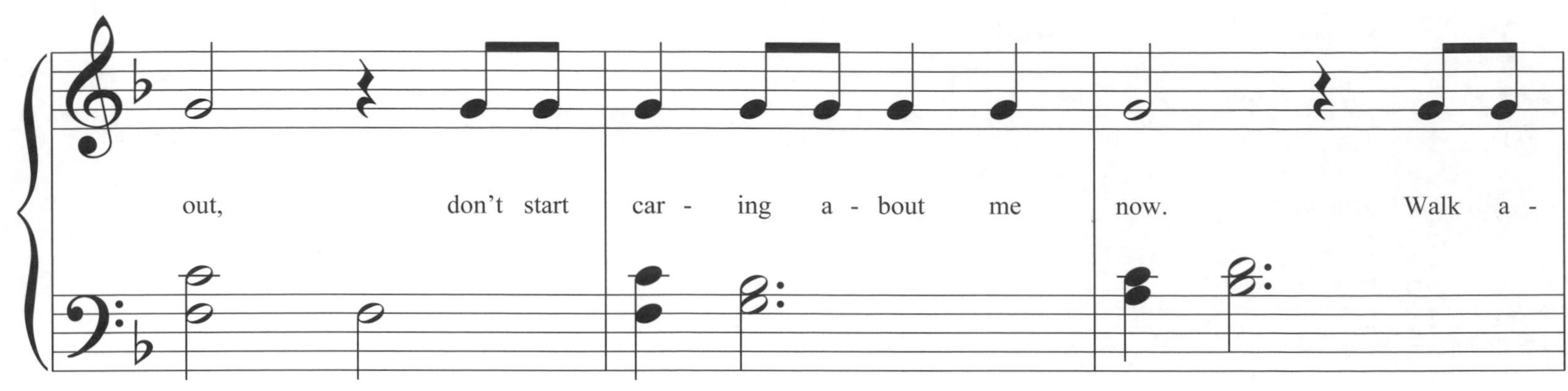
out, don't start
car - ing a - bout me
now. Walk a -

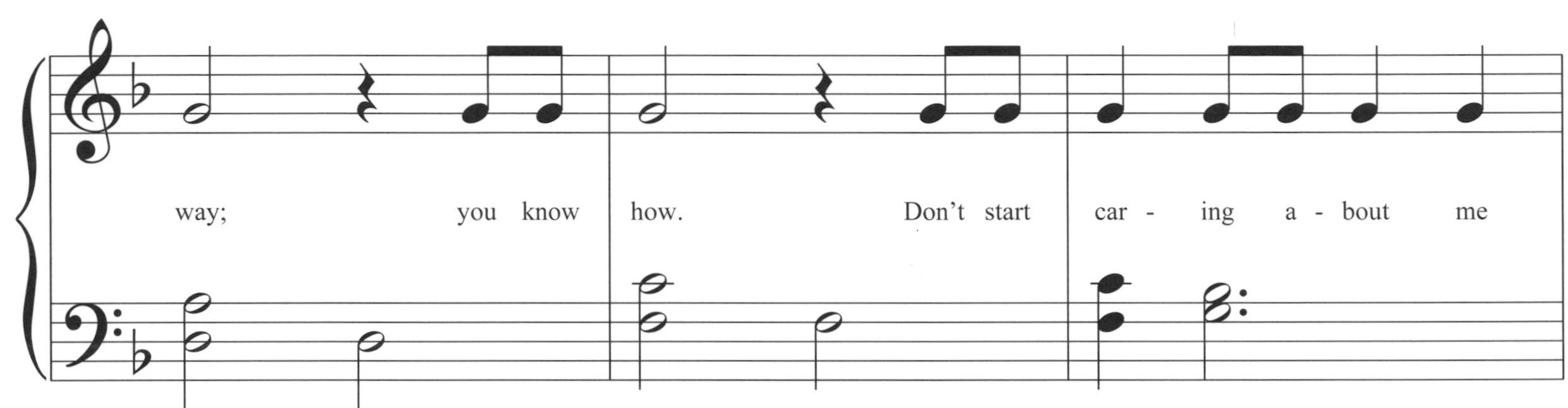
way; you know
how. Don't start
car - ing a - bout me

now. (So...
Up, up,
don't come out.

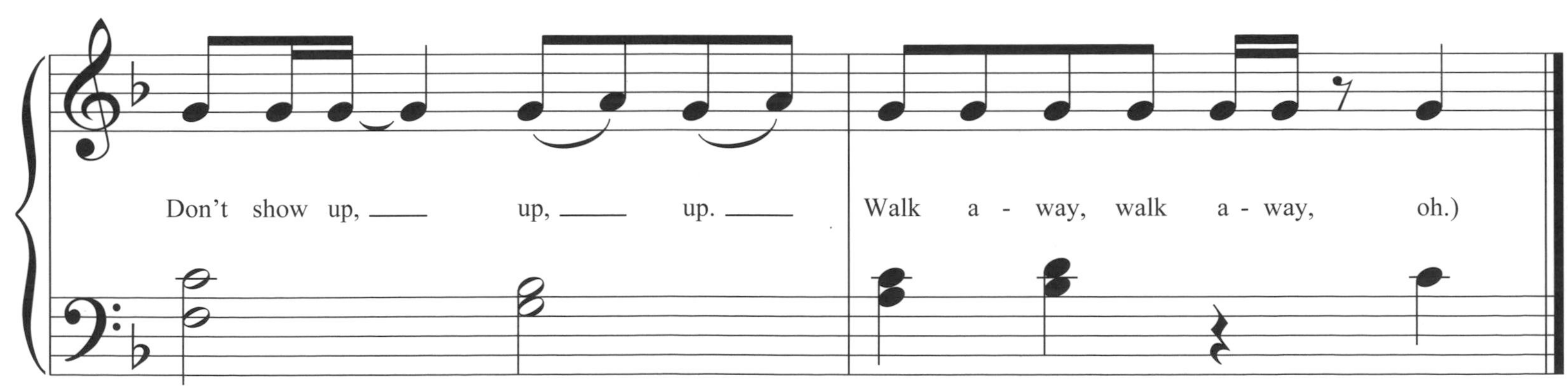
Don't show up, up, up.
Walk a - way, walk a - way, oh.)

CIRCLES

Words and Music by AUSTIN POST,
KAAN GUNESBERK, LOUIS BELL,
WILLIAM WALSH and ADAM FEENEY

Moderately fast

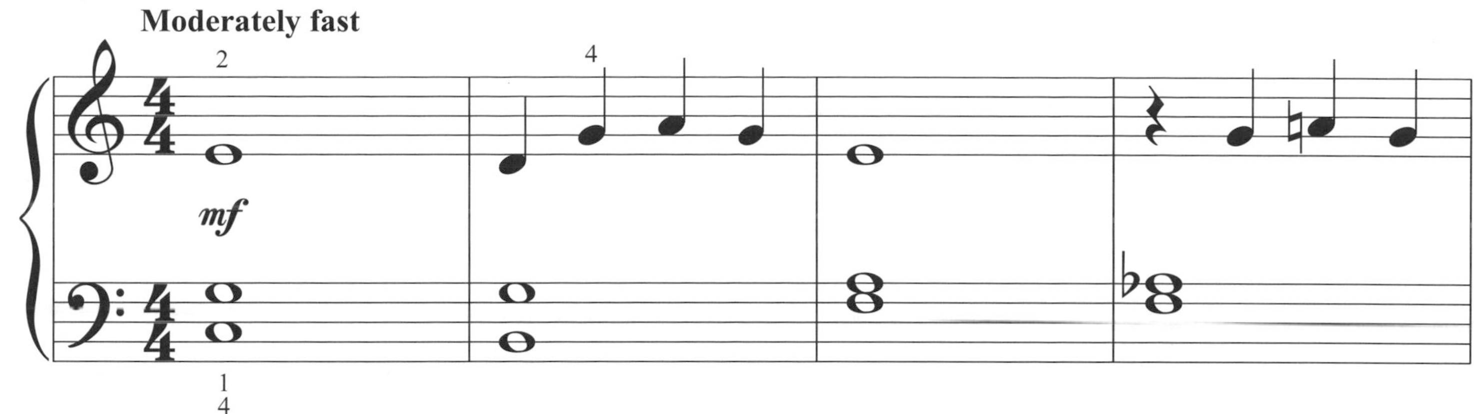

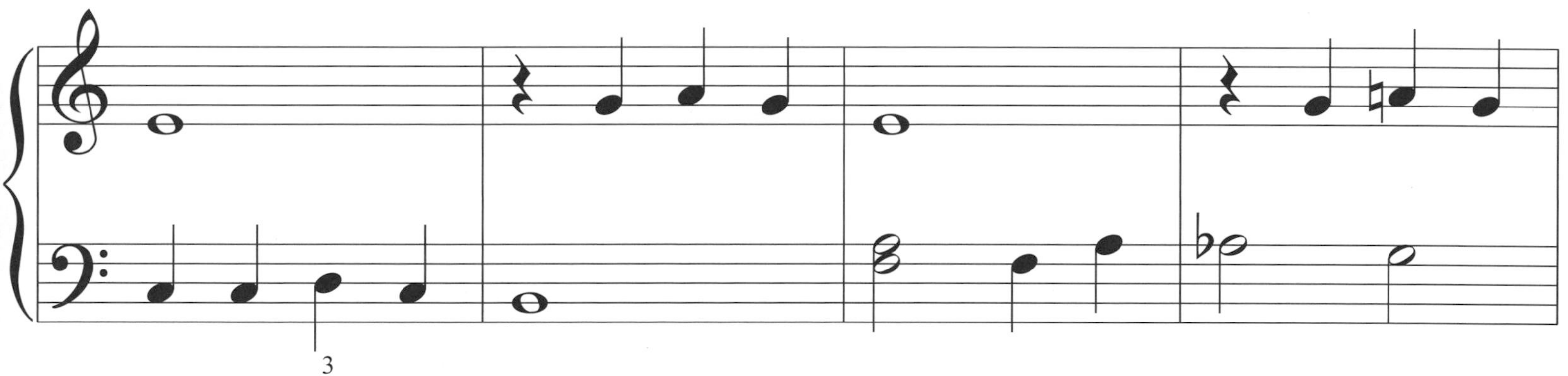

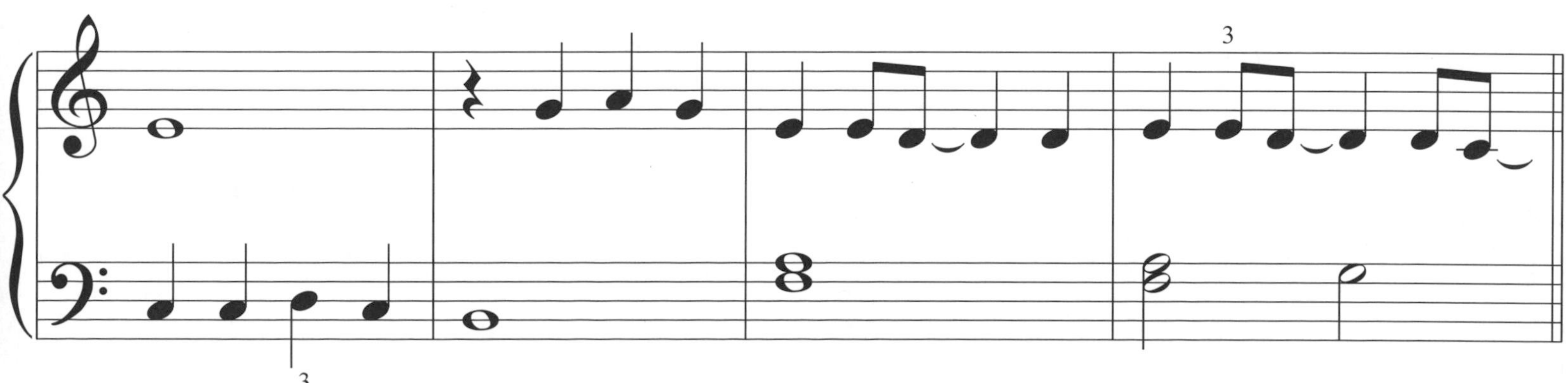

4
We could - n't turn a - round
3

'til we were up - side
down.
I'll be the bad guy
3

now,
but no, I ain't too
proud.
4

3
I could - n't be there.
E - ven when I

5
try,
you don't be - lieve it.
4

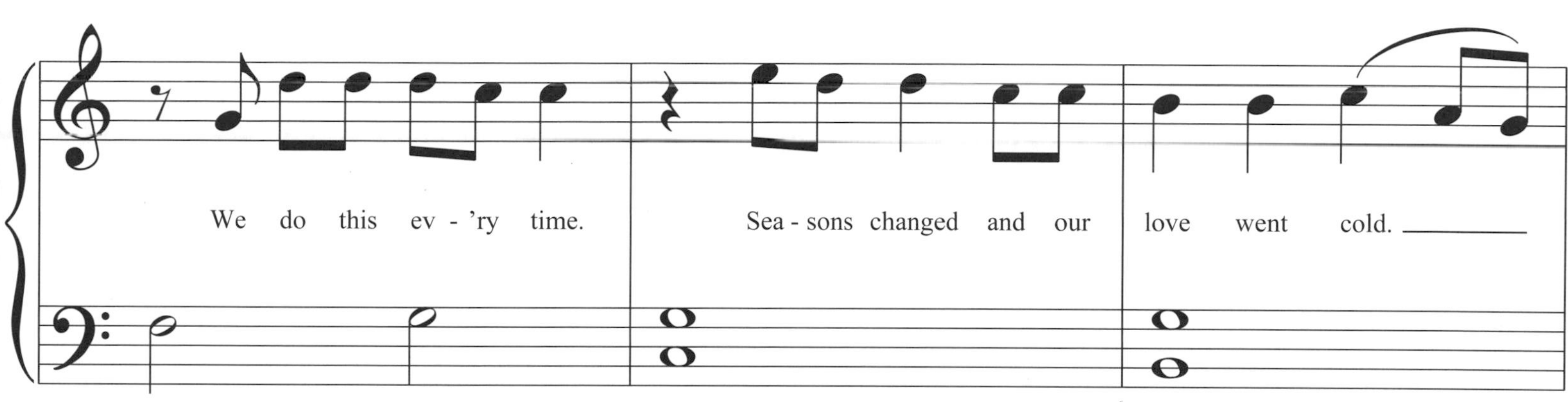
We do this ev - 'ry time.
Sea - sons changed and our
love went cold.

Feed the flame 'cause we
can't let go.
Run a - way, but we're

run - ning in cir - cles.
Run a - way, run
3
a - way. I dare you to

do some - thing
I'm wait - ing on
you a - gain

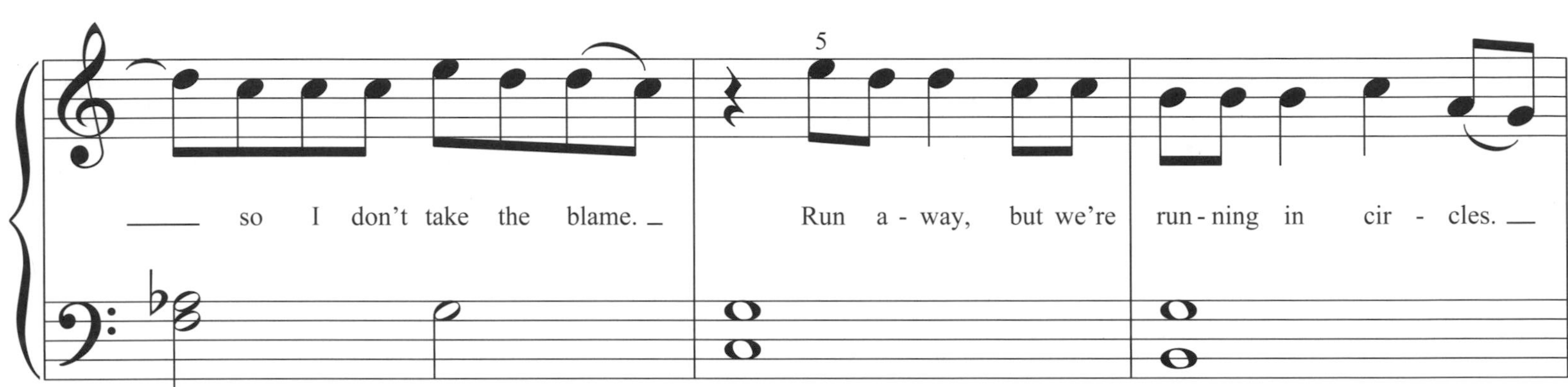
so I don't take the blame.
5
Run a - way, but we're
run - ning in cir - cles.

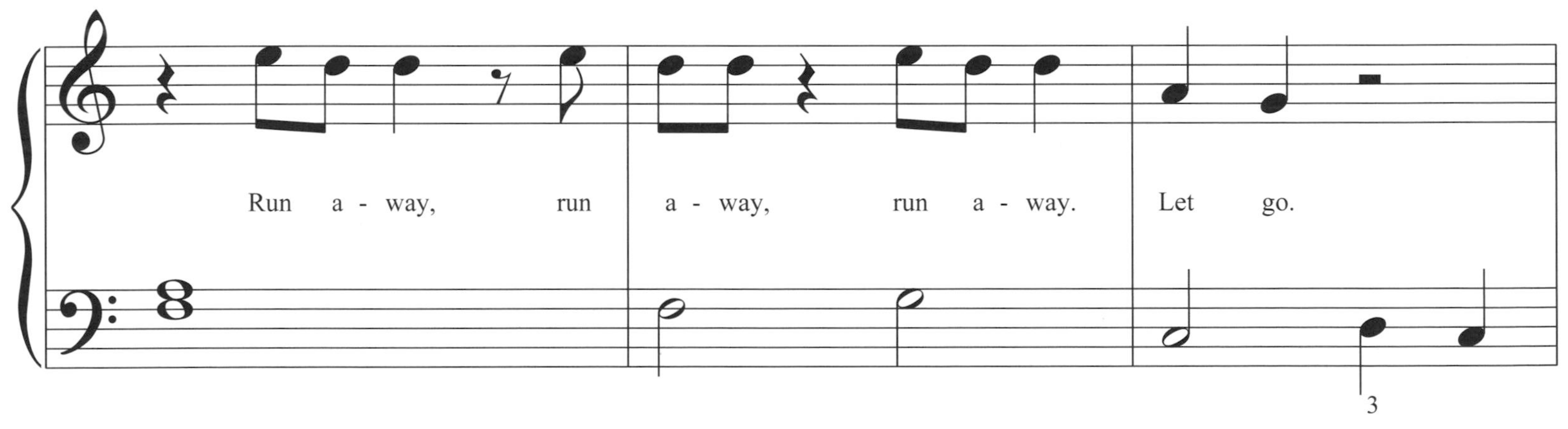
Run a - way, run
a - way, run a - way.
Let go.
3

5
I got a feel - ing that it's
time to let go.
I

say so. I knew that this was doomed from the get - go.
4

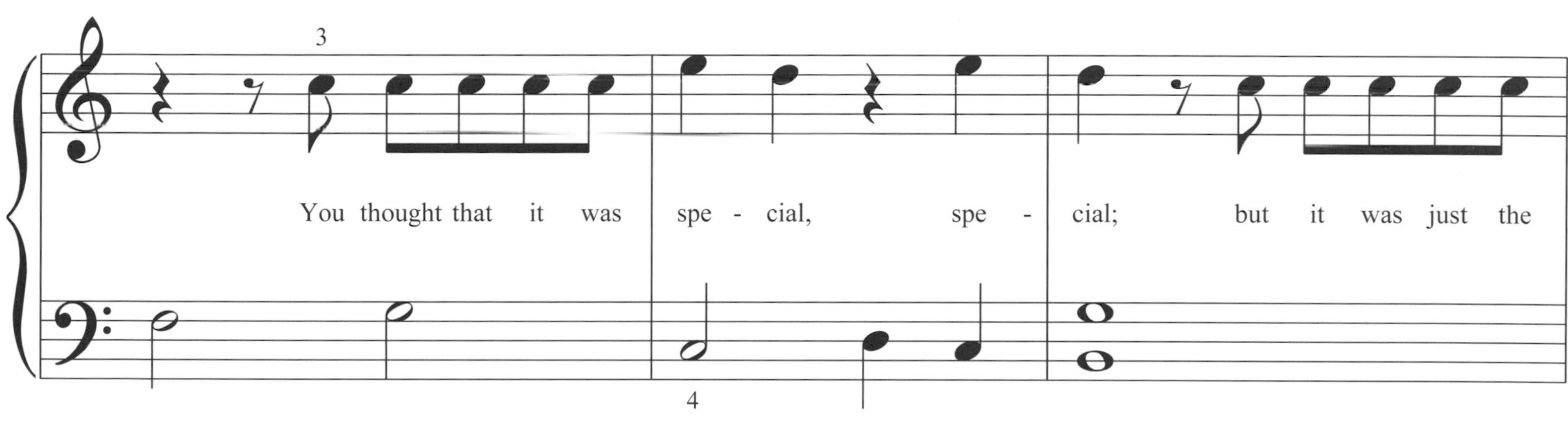
3
You thought that it was spe - cial, spe - cial; but it was just the
4

sex, oh, the sex, though. And I still hear the ech - oes, the ech -
4

4
1
oes. I got a feel - ing that it's time to let it go. Let it go.

Sea - sons changed and our love went cold. Feed the flame 'cause we

can't let go. Run a - way, but we're run - ning in cir - cles.

3
Run a - way, run a - way. I dare you to do some - thing.

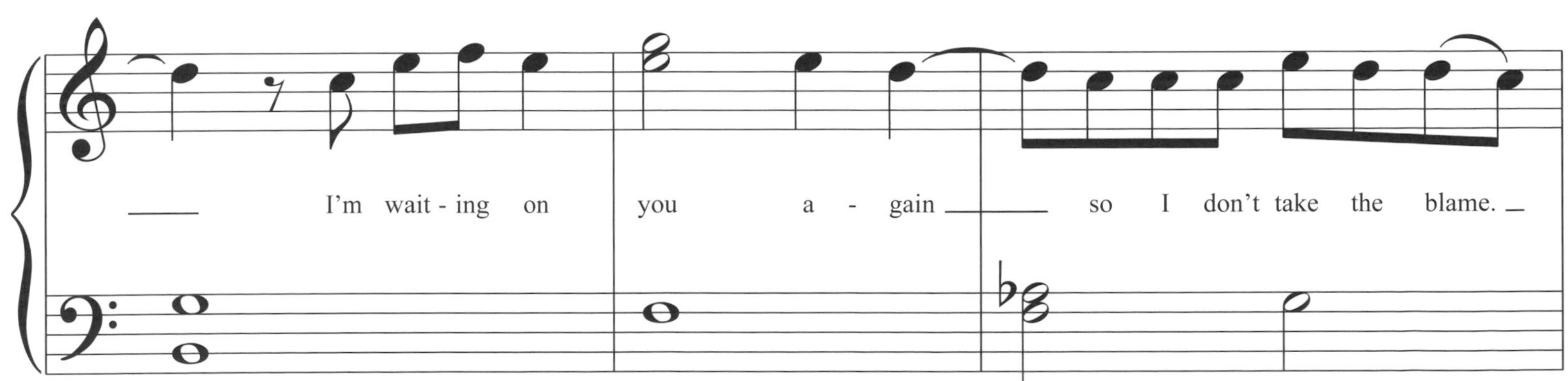
I'm wait - ing on you a - gain so I don't take the blame.

5
Run a - way, but we're run - ning in cir - cles.
Run a - way, run

1.
4
a - way, run a - way. May - be you don't un - der - stand what I'm go - ing through.

It's on - ly me; what you got to lose? Make up your mind. Tell me,

2.
1
what are you gon - na do? It's on - ly me. Let it go.

EVERYTHING I WANTED

Words and Music by BILLIE EILISH O'CONNELL
and FINNEAS O'CONNELL

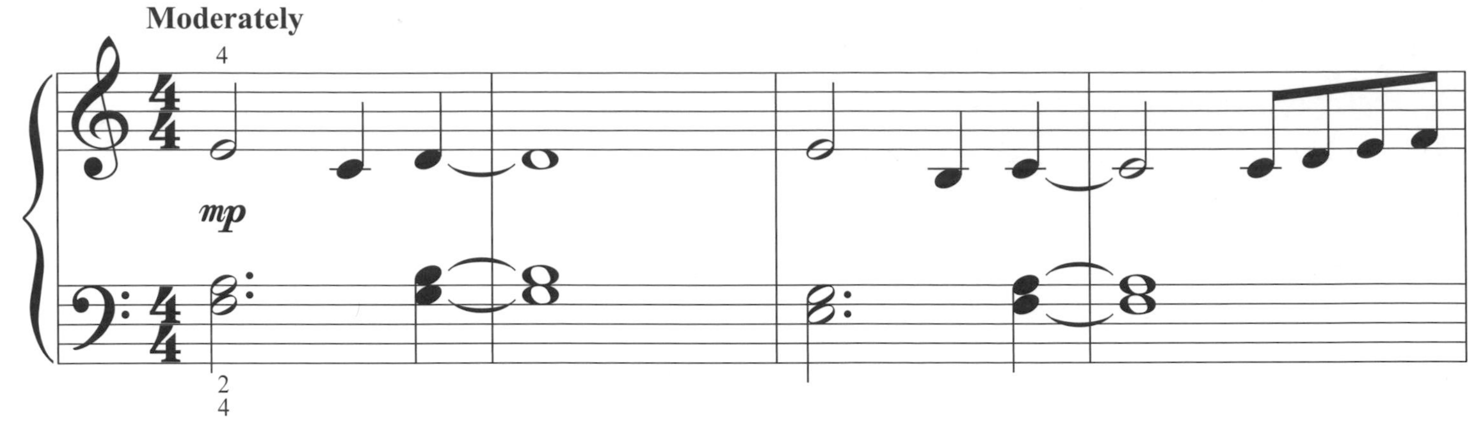

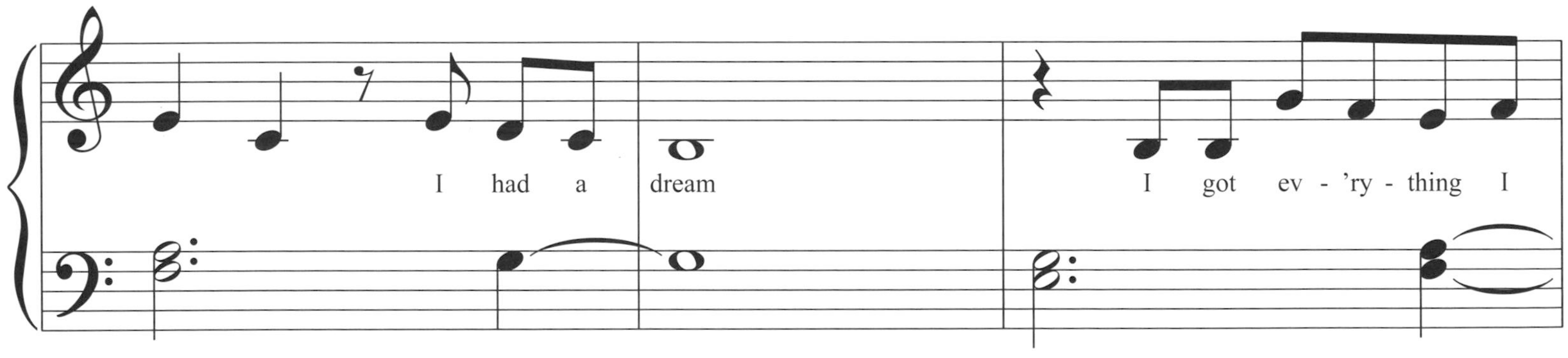

5
2
hon - est, it might have been a night - mare to an - y - one who

2
might care. Thought I could

fly, so I stepped off the Gold - en, mm.

4
No - bod - y cried, no - bod - y e - ven

5
noticed. I saw them stand - ing
right there,
5
kind - a thought they

might care.
𝄋
4
I had a

dream
I got ev - 'ry - thing I
want - ed.
But

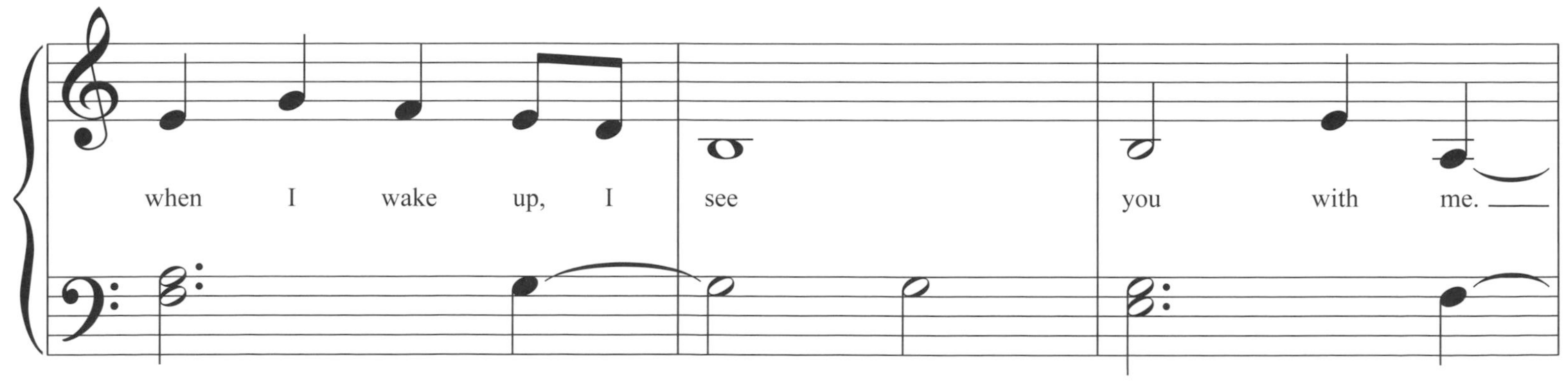
when I wake up, I
see
you with me.

3
And you say, “As long as I’m here,
4
no one can hurt you.
3
Don’t want to
lie here, but you can learn to.
3
If I could
change the way that you see your - self,

3
3
you would - n't won - der
why you're here.
They don't de - serve

To Coda
4
you."
I tried to
scream,

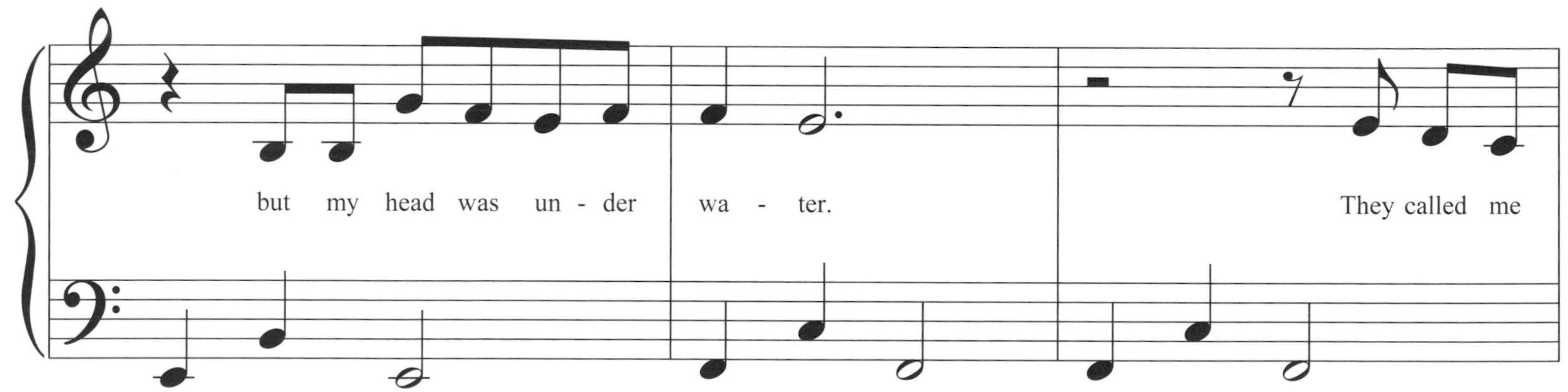
but my head was un - der
wa - ter.
They called me

weak,
like I'm not just some - bod - y's
daugh - ter. It could have been a

2
night - mare,
but it felt like they were
right there.

1
And it
feels like yes - ter - day was a
year a - go, but

I don't want to let an - y -
bod - y know. 'Cause
ev - 'ry - bod - y wants some - thing

D.S. al Coda
from me now, and
I don't want to let them down.

CODA
3
If I knew it all then, would I do it a - gain,

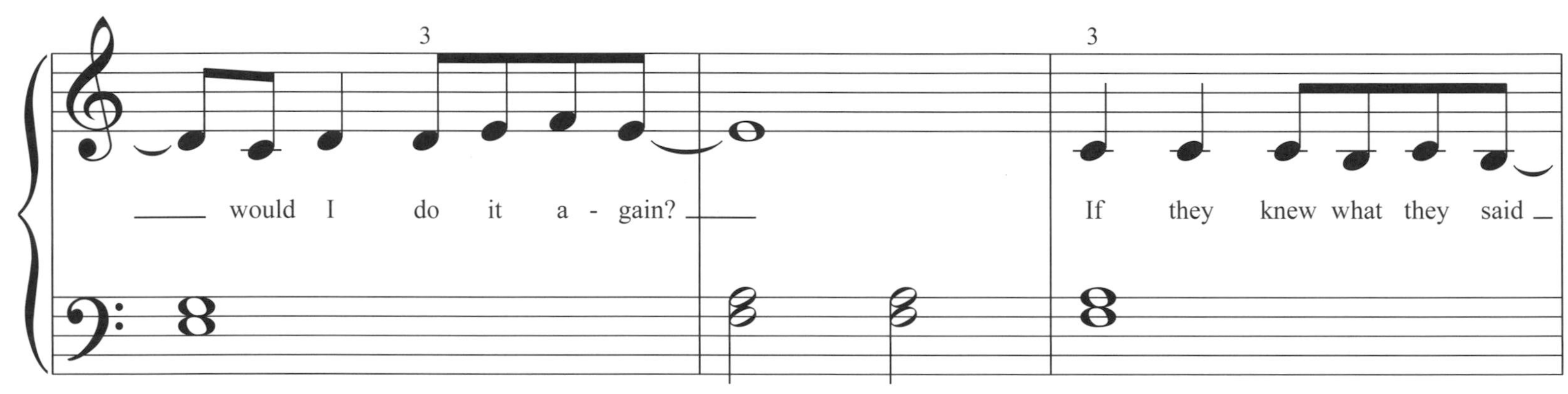
3
would I do it a - gain?
3
If they knew what they said

would go straight to my head,
3
what would they say in - stead?

p
4

GOOD AS HELL

Words and Music by LIZZO
and ERIC FREDERIC

5
Come now, come dry your eyes. You know you're a star, you can touch the sky. I know that it's
Boss up and change your life. You can have it all, no sac - ri - fice. I know he did you

hard, but you have to try. If you need ad - vice, let me sim - pli - fy. If
wrong; we can make it right, so go and let it all hang out to - night. 'Cause

he don't love you an - y - more, just walk your fine self out the door. I do my
he don't love you an - y - more, so walk your fine self out the door and do your

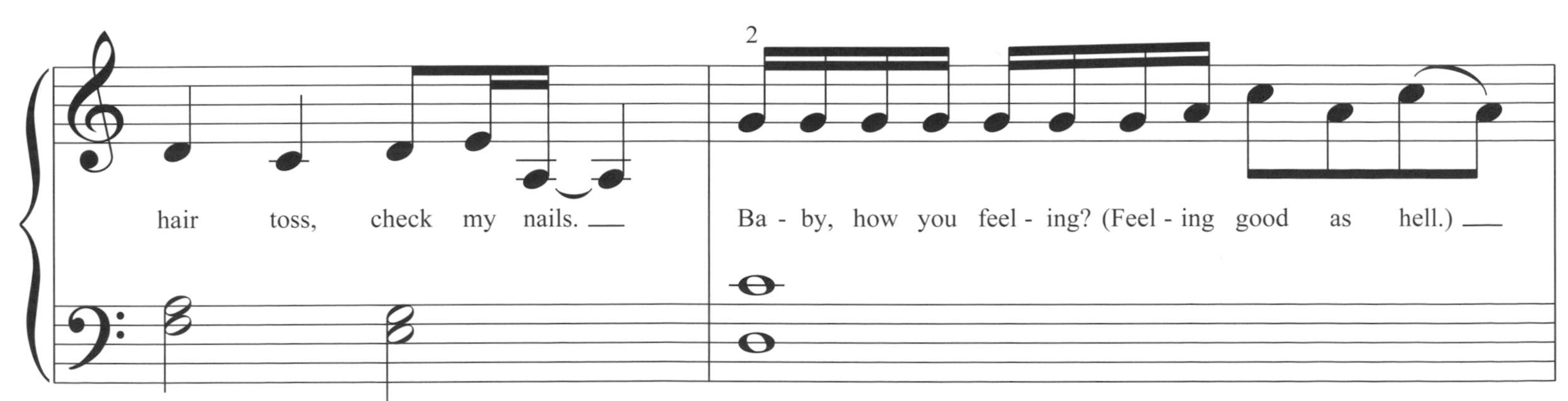
2
hair toss, check my nails. Ba - by, how you feel - ing? (Feel - ing good as hell.)

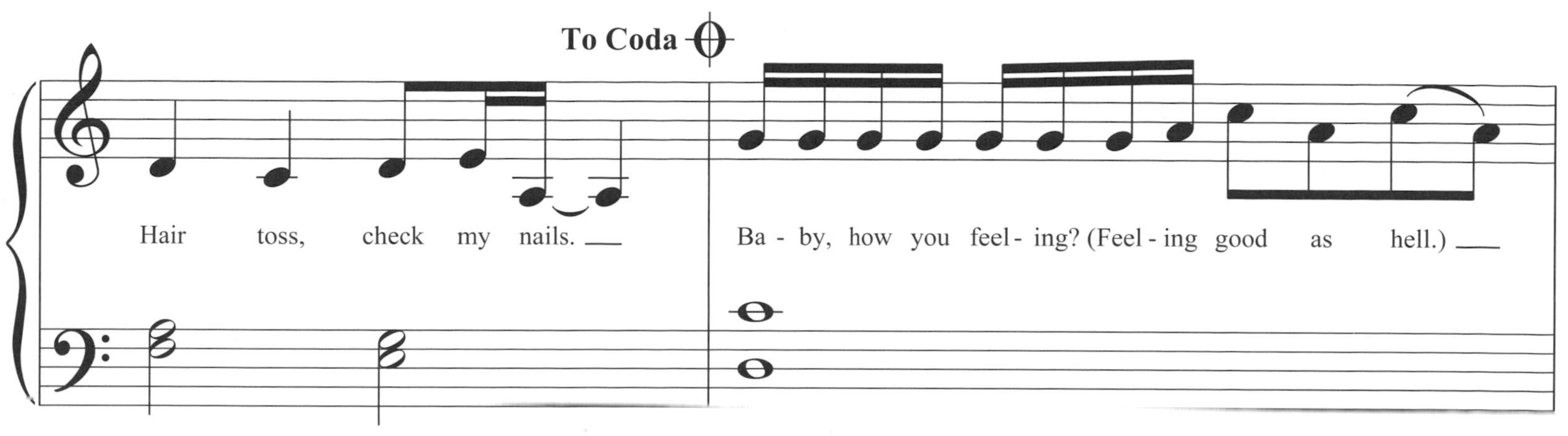
To Coda
Hair toss, check my nails.
Ba - by, how you feel - ing? (Feel - ing good as hell.)

(Feel - ing good as hell.)
2
Ba - by, how you feel - ing? (Feel - ing good as hell.)

3
Woo, girl, need to kick off your shoes. Got - ta
take a deep breath, time to fo - cus on you. All the

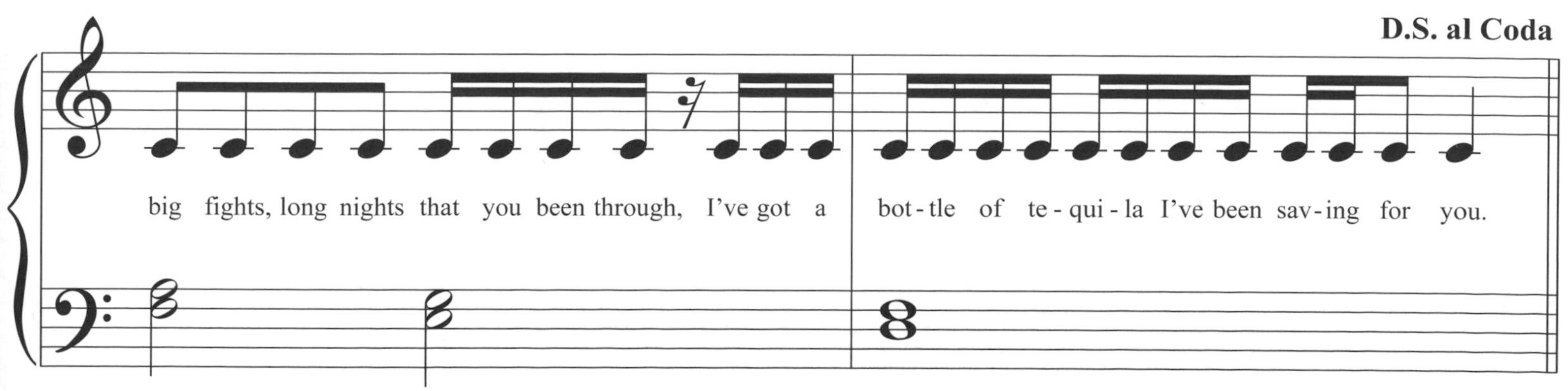
D.S. al Coda
big fights, long nights that you been through, I've got a
bot - tle of te - qui - la I've been sav - ing for you.

CODA

3
Ba - by, how you feel - ing? (Feel - ing good as hell.)
Hair toss, check my nails.

Ba - by, how you feel - ing? (Feel - ing good as hell.)
Hair toss, check my nails.

Ba - by, how you feel - ing? (Feel - ing good as hell.)
Hmm,

yeah,
al - right.
Lis - ten: If
he don't love you an - y - more,

then
walk your fine self out the door.
And do your

hair toss, check my nails.
Ba - by, how you feel - ing? (Feel - ing good as hell.)

Hair toss, check my nails.
Ba - by, how you feel - ing? (Feel - ing good as hell.)

(Feel - ing good as hell.)
Ba - by, how you feel - ing? (Feel - ing good as hell.)

HEY LOOK MA, I MADE IT

Words and Music by BRENDON URIE,
DILLON FRANCIS, SAMUEL HOLLANDER,
MICHAEL ANGELAKOS, JACOB SINCLAIR
and MORGAN KIBBY

do the deed, get up and leave, a climb - er and a sa - dist, yeah.
nev - er know who you can trust, then trust me, you'll be lone - ly, oh.
3
Are you read - y for the se - quel?
Ain't read - y for the lat - est?
In the gar - den of e - vil,
I'm gon - na be the great - est.
1
In a gold - en ca - the - dral.
I'll be pray - ing for the faith - less. And

if you lose, boo - hoo. Hey, look, Ma, I made it. Hey, look Ma, I

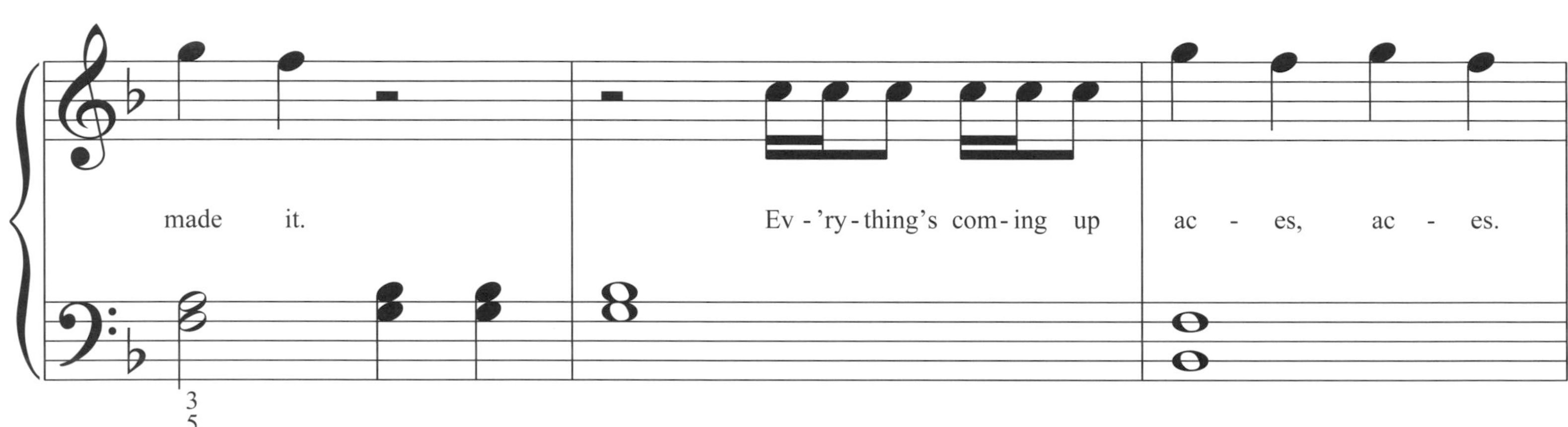
made it. Ev - 'ry - thing's com - ing up ac - es, ac - es.
3
5

If it's a dream, don't wake me, don't wake me. I said, "Hey, look Ma, I

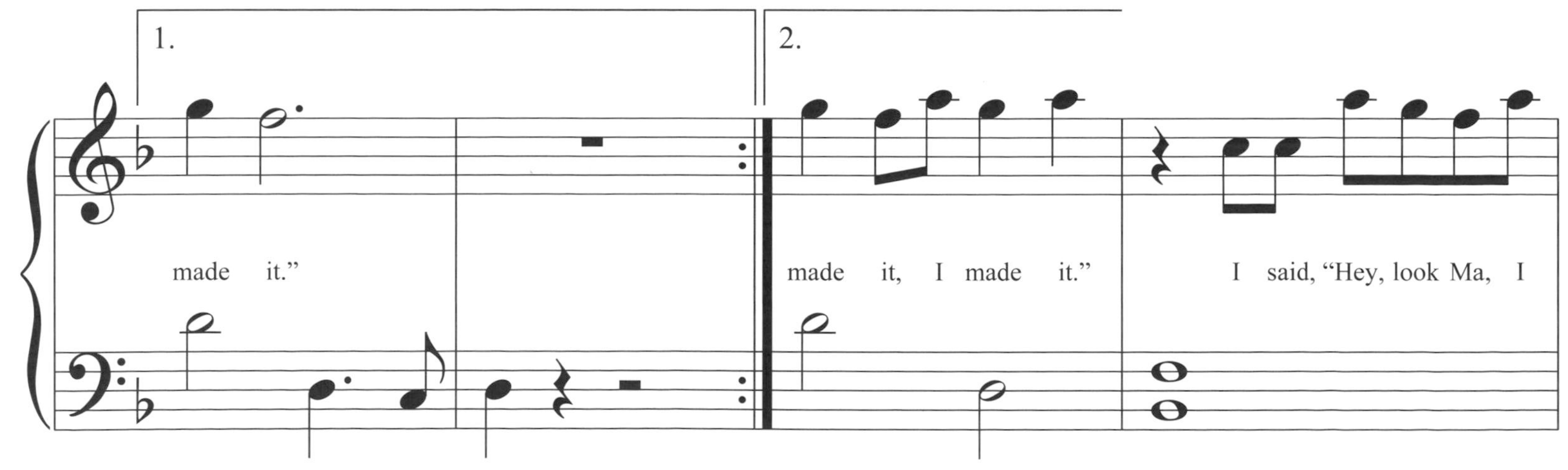
1.
2.
made it." made it, I made it." I said, "Hey, look Ma, I

made it, I made it."
I see it, I want it, I
take it, take it.

If it's a dream, don't
wake me, don't wake me.
I said, "Hey, look Ma, I

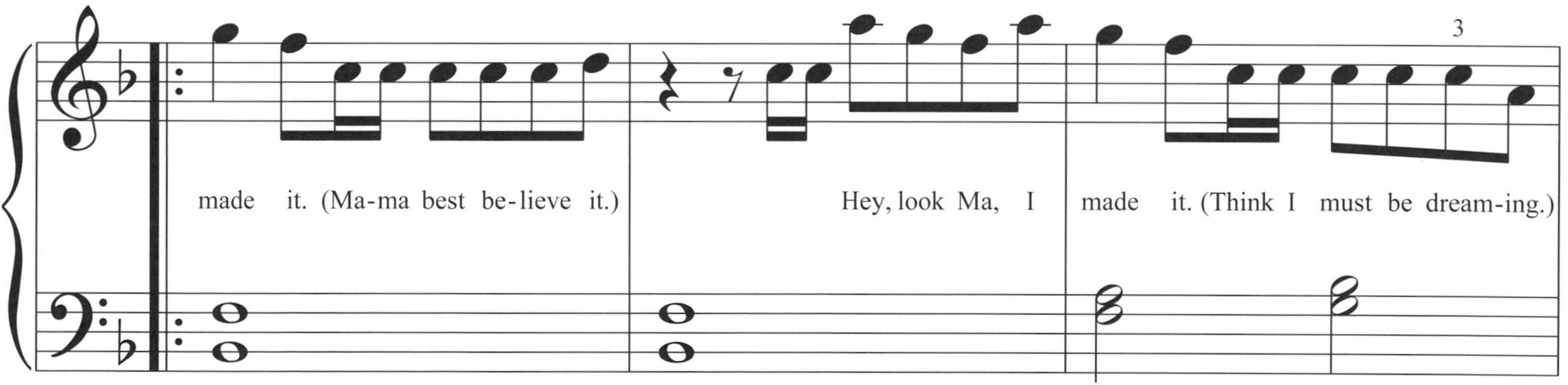
made it. (Ma-ma best be-lieve it.)
Hey, look Ma, I
made it. (Think I must be dream-ing.)
3

1.
2.
Hey, look Ma, I
Hey, look Ma, I
made it."

THE HYPE

Words and Music by PAUL MEANY
and TYLER JOSEPH

Moderate Pop beat

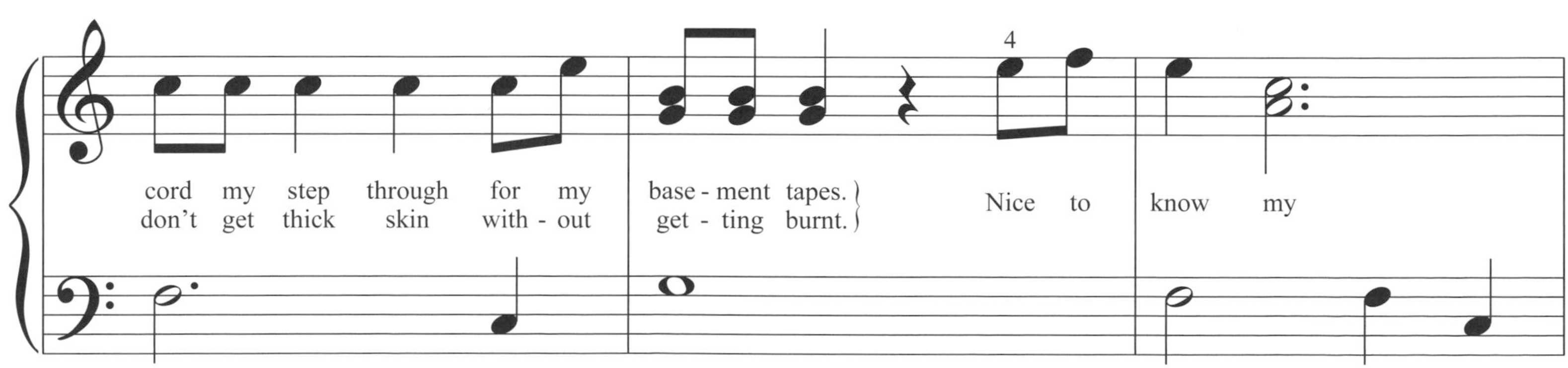

4
kind will be on my side. I don't be - lieve the hype. And you

know you're a ter - ri - ble sight, but you'll be just fine. Just don't be - lieve the

1.
2.
hype. Yeah, hype.

4
No,

4
I don't know which way I'm go - ing,
but
I can hear my way a - round.

No,
I don't know which way I'm go - ing,
but
1
2

4
I can hear my way a - round.
No,
I don't know which way I'm go - ing,

2
but
I can hear my way a - round.
Oh,

4
I can hear my way a - round.
Nice to
know my
kind will be on my

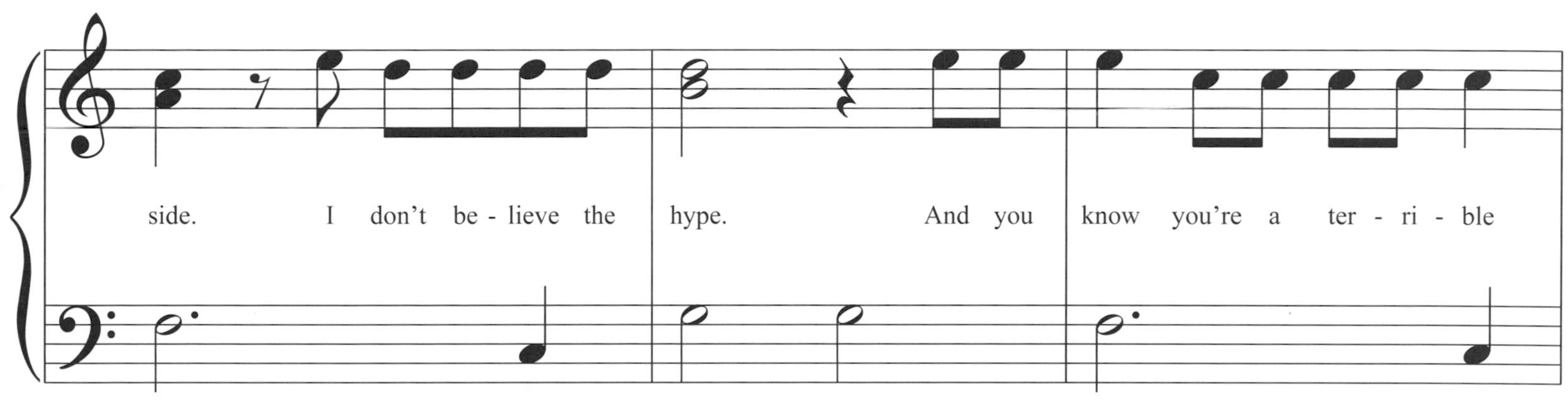
side. I don't be - lieve the
hype. And you
know you're a ter - ri - ble

sight, but you'll be just
fine. Just don't be - lieve the
hype. Nice to

know my
4
kind will be on my
side. I don't be - lieve the

hype. And you
know you're a ter - ri - ble
sight, but you'll be just

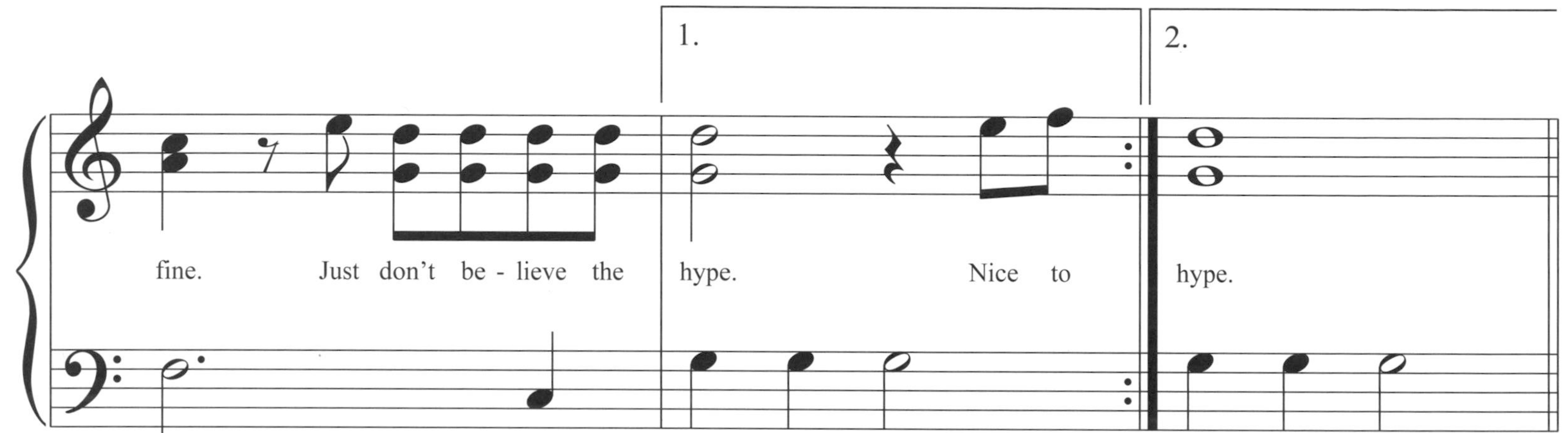
1.
2.
fine. Just don't be - lieve the
hype. Nice to
hype.

1.
5
2

2.
5
2

ONLY HUMAN

Words and Music by NICK JONAS,
JOSEPH JONAS, SHELLBACK
and KEVIN JONAS

4
You got all my love to spend. Let's find
a place where hap - pi - ness be - gins.
3
We gon'
dance in the liv - ing room, slave to the way you move.
3
Hurts when I'm leav - in' you, ay. Just
3
dance in the liv - ing room, love with an at - ti - tude.
3
Drunk to an eight - ies groove, ay. We gon'

dance in the liv-ing room, slave to the way you move. Hurts when I'm leav-in' you, ay.
Dance in the liv-ing room, love with an at-ti-tude, drunk. It's on-ly
hu - man, you know that it's real. So why would you fight or try to de-ny the way that you
feel? Oh babe, you can't fool me. Your bod-y's got oth - er plans so

To Coda
3
stop pre - tend - ing you're shy, just come on and
dance, dance, dance, dance,

oh.

Ear - ly morn- in' la - la
light.

On - ly get - tin' up to close the blinds.
Oh,

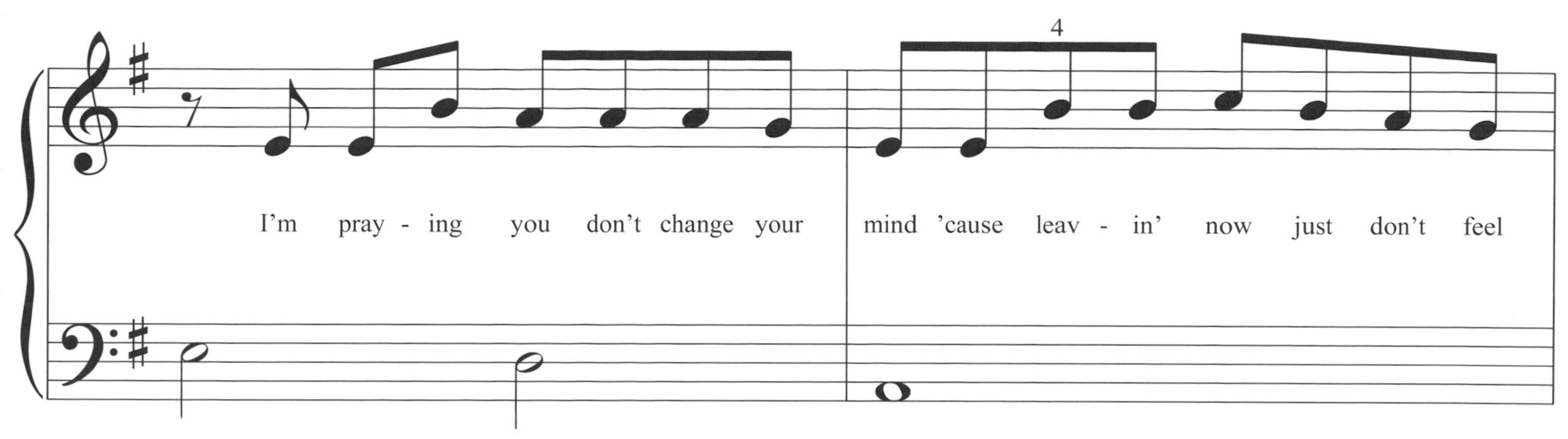
4
I'm pray - ing you don't change your
mind 'cause leav - in' now just don't feel

D.S. al Coda
right. Let's do it one more
time. We gon'

CODA
oh.
On - ly hu -

3
3
man. It's on-ly man, it's on-ly
man, on - ly hu - man.

LIFE IN THE CITY

Words and Music by JEREMY FRAITES
and WESLEY SCHULTZ

4
3 1 2
dream, it died; J - M - Z line, Myr - tle and Broad - way. But I'd be glad to see Man - hat - tan for once.

Whoa, whoa, liv - ing life in the cit - y, whoa, whoa,

it will nev - er be pret - ty. Oh. Oh.

Whoa, whoa, we can plan if we make it. Whoa, whoa,

To Coda
3
we won't let 'em, they won't take it from me.
No, oh, oh, whoa.

(Two, three, four.)
Woo, woo.
4

2
Woo, woo.
And if you
leave, don't leave me all a -
2
4

lone; 'cause I'll be
scared, I'll be na - ked, I'll be cold.

And I miss my dad and Cle - o - pat - ra

sit-ting on the phone. So take me back off these streets and we'll

3
nev - er be a - part, to - geth - er from the start, nev - er, nev - er

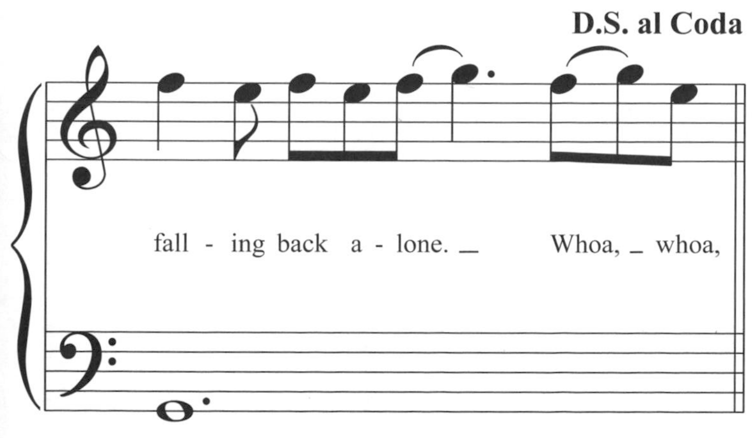
D.S. al Coda
fall - ing back a - lone. Whoa, whoa,

CODA
1 2
And if the

sun don't shine on me to - day, and if the
da da da da da da. Da da da
sub - ways flood and bridg - es break, will you just
da da da da da da. Da da da
1 2 3
lay down and dig your grave, or will you
da da da da da da. Da da da
rail a - gainst your dy - ing day? Da da da
da da da da da da.
1.
2.

TRUTH HURTS

Words and Music by LIZZO,
ERIC FREDERIC, JESSE ST. JOHN GELLER
and STEVEN CHEUNG

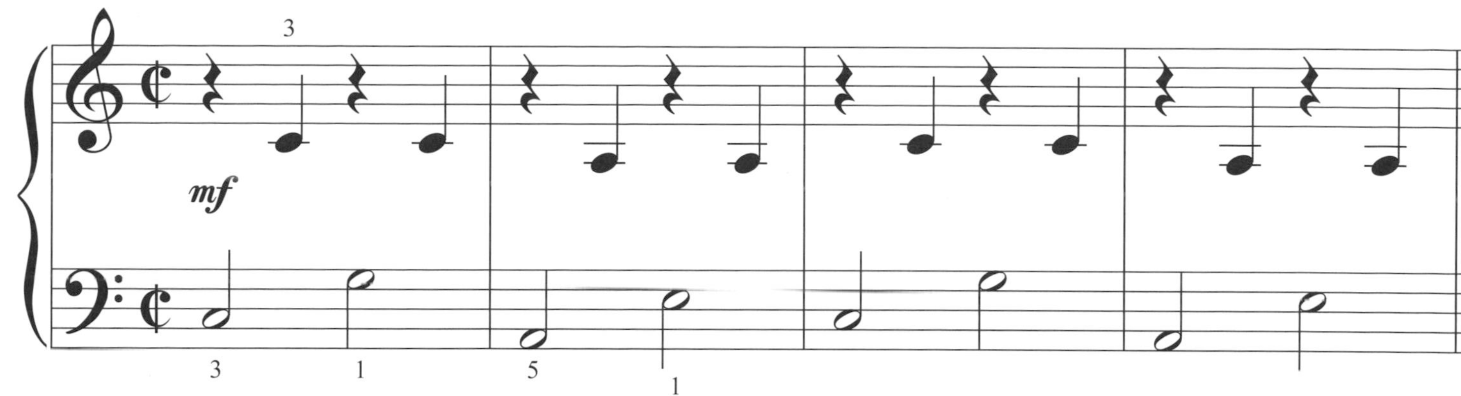

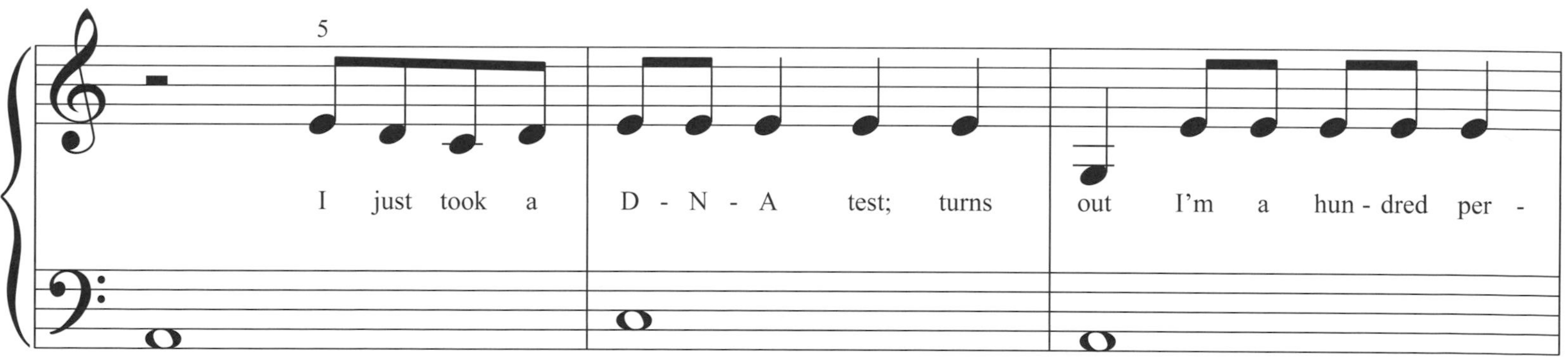

5
hu - man in me. Bling,
bling, then I solve 'em, that's the
5
god - dess in me.
You could - a had a

good friend, non - com -
mit - tal. Help you with your
ca - reer just a

lit - tle. You're 'posed to hold me
down, but you're
2
hold - in' me back. And that's the

sound of me not
call - ing you back.
Why men great

5
5
'til they got - ta be great?
Don't text me,
tell it straight to my face.
Best friend sat me

down in the sa - lon chair.
Sham - poo press,
get you out - ta my hair.
Fresh pho - tos

with the bomb light - ing.
New man on the
Min - ne - so - ta Vi - kings.
Truth hurts, need - ed

some-thing more ex - cit - ing.
Bom, bom, bi, bom, bi,
bum, bum, bay. You tried to

3
5
break my heart. Oh, that breaks my heart that you thought you ev - er had it. No, you

ain't from the start. Hey, I'm glad you're back with your friends. I mean, who would wan - na hide this? I will

1 2
nev - er, ev - er, ev - er, ev - er be your side chick. I put the sing in

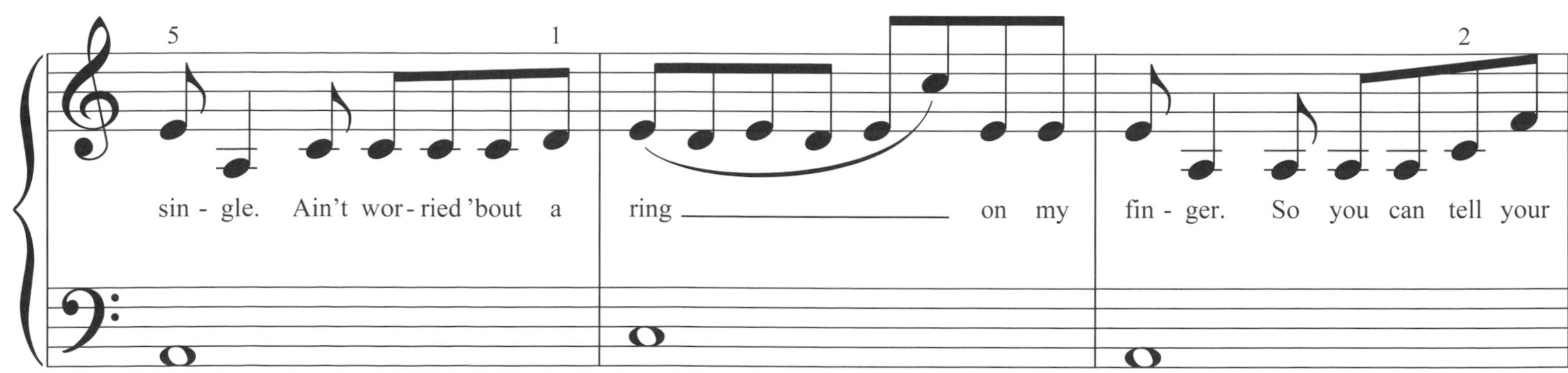
5
1
2
sin - gle. Ain't wor - ried 'bout a ring on my fin - ger. So you can tell your

friend, "Shoot your shot when you see 'em." It's o - kay, he al -

5
read - y knows my feel - ings. Why men great 'til they got - ta be great?
5

Don't text me, tell it straight to my face. Best friend sat me
5

down in the sa - lon chair. Sham - poo press, get you out - ta my hair.

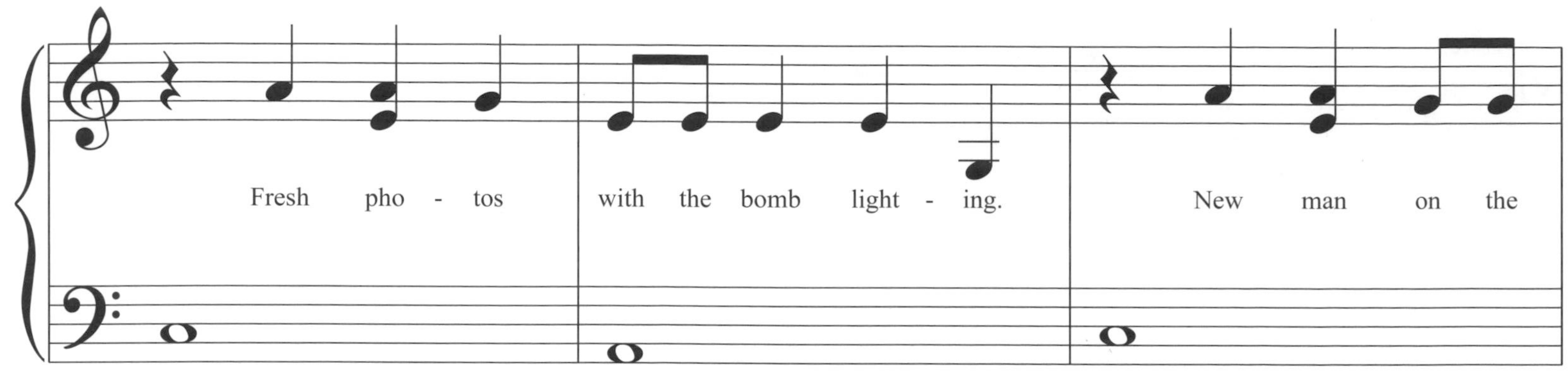
Fresh pho - tos
with the bomb light - ing.
New man on the

Min - ne - so - ta Vi - kings.
Truth hurts, need - ed
some-thing more ex - cit - ing.

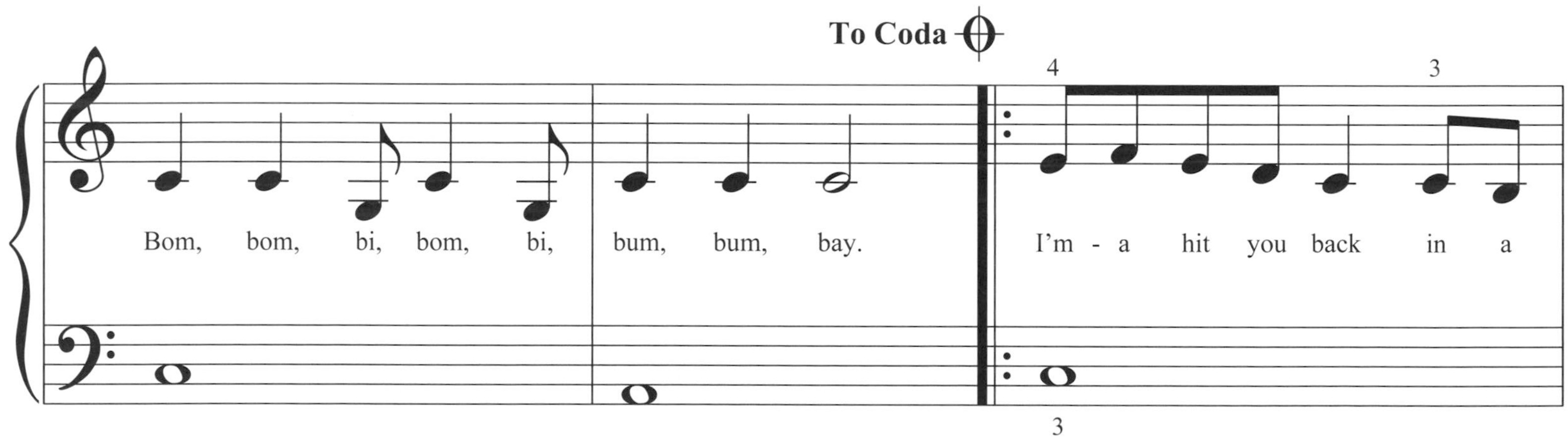
To Coda
4
3
Bom, bom, bi, bom, bi,
bum, bum, bay.
I'm - a hit you back in a
3

4
3
min - ute.
I don't play tag, yeah, I
been it.

We don't deal with lies,
we don't do good-byes.
We just keep it push - in' like

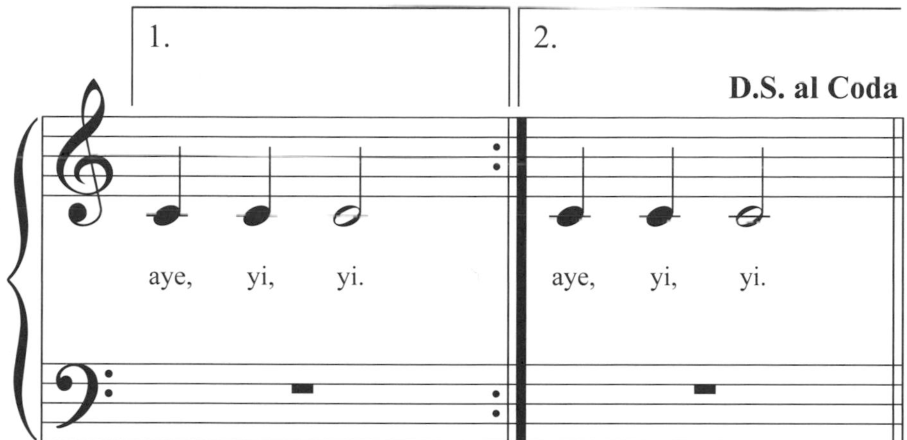
1.
2.
D.S. al Coda
aye, yi, yi.
aye, yi, yi.

CODA

With the bomb
light - ing.
Min - ne - so - ta

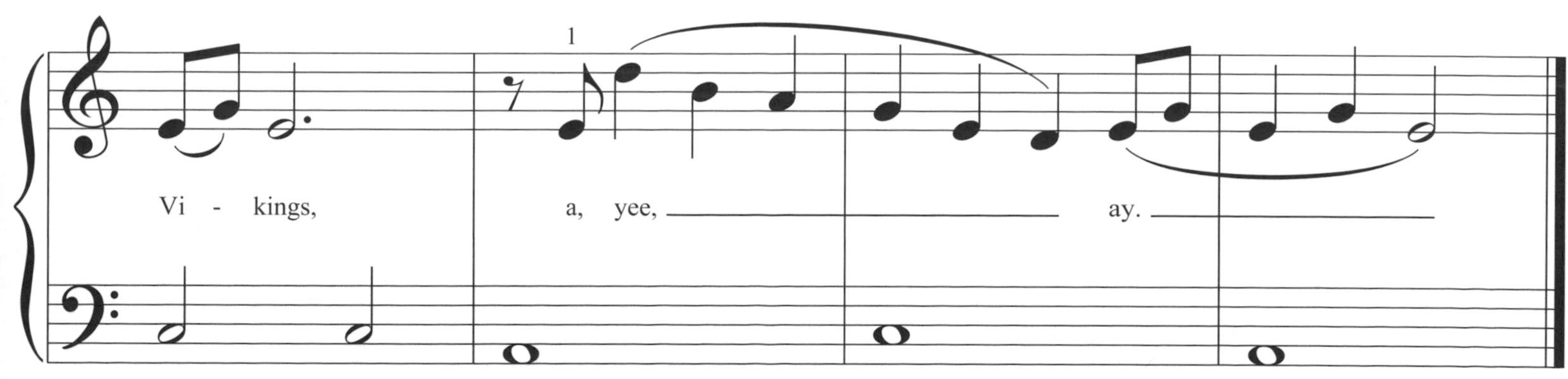
Vi - kings,
a, yee,
ay.

LOSE YOU TO LOVE ME

Words and Music by SELENA GOMEZ,
JUSTIN TRANTER, JULIA MICHAELS,
ROBIN FREDRIKSSON and MATTIAS LARSSON

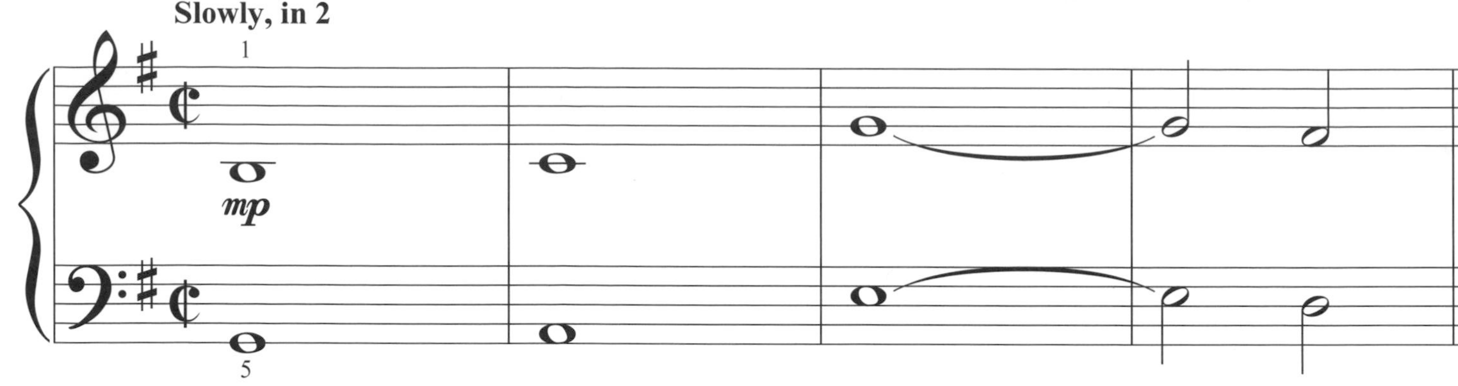

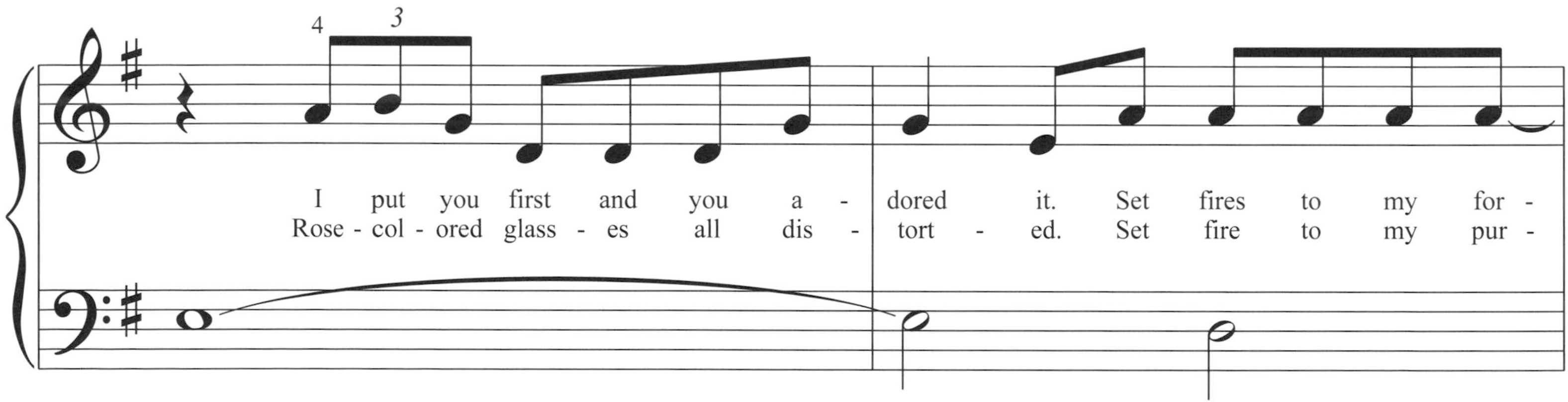

1.
2.
- rus 'cause it was - n't yours.
- ing when it was - n't yours,
yeah.

3
We'd al - ways go in - to it blind - ly.
I need - ed to lose

you to find me.
This dance, it was kill - ing me soft - ly.

I need - ed to hate you to love me, yeah.
To love, love, yeah, to

3
love, love, yeah, to love, yeah. I need - ed to lose ___ you to love me, yeah.

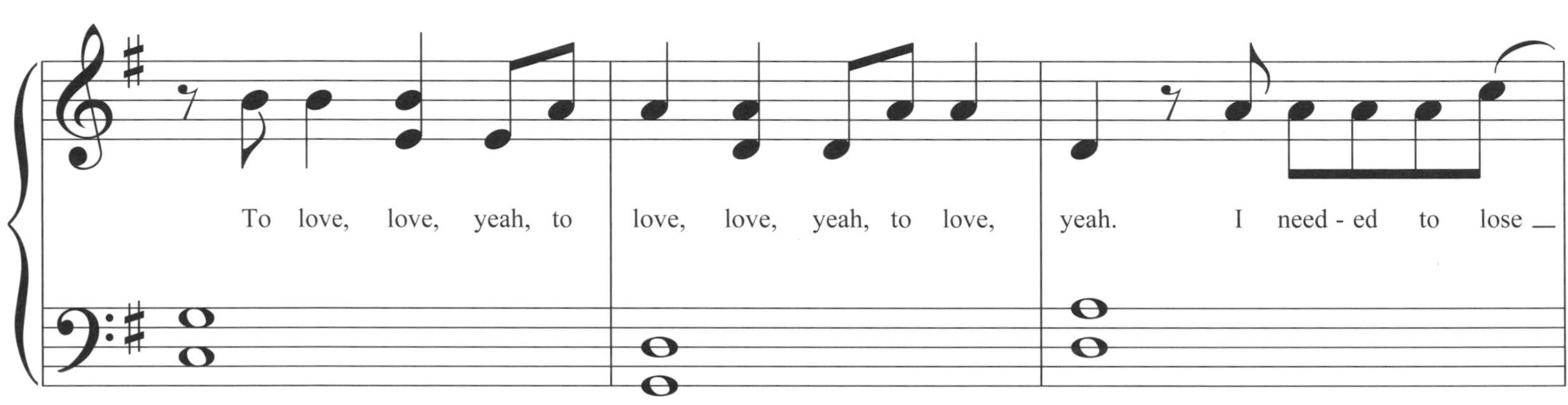
To love, love, yeah, to love, love, yeah, to love, yeah. I need - ed to lose ___

To Coda
3
___ you to love me. I gave my all and they all know it.

3
Then you tore me down and now it's show - ing. In two months you re - placed ___

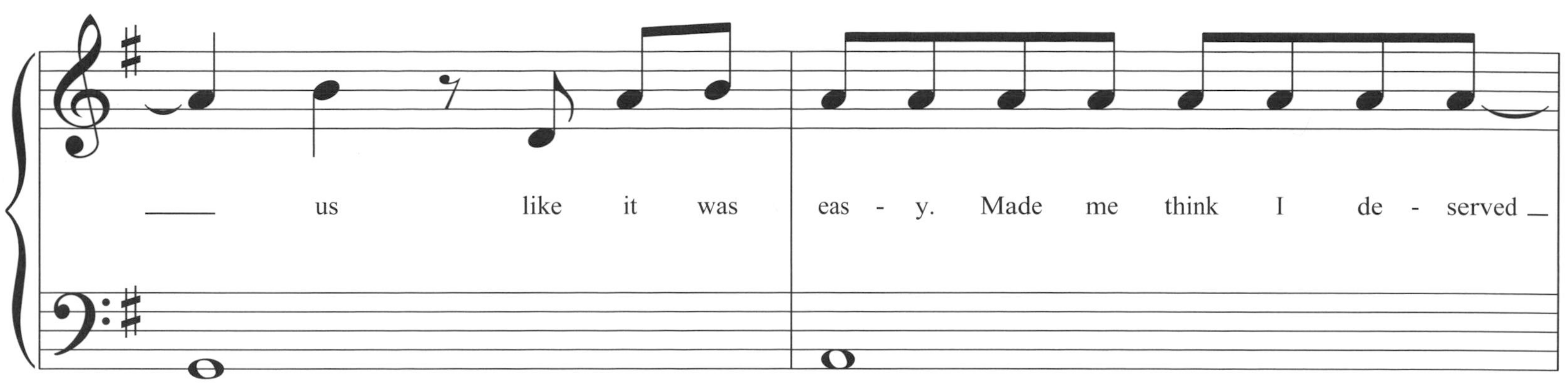

us like it was
eas - y. Made me think I de - served

D.S. al Coda
it in the thick of heal - ing, yeah.

CODA
3
You prom - ised the world and I fell for it.

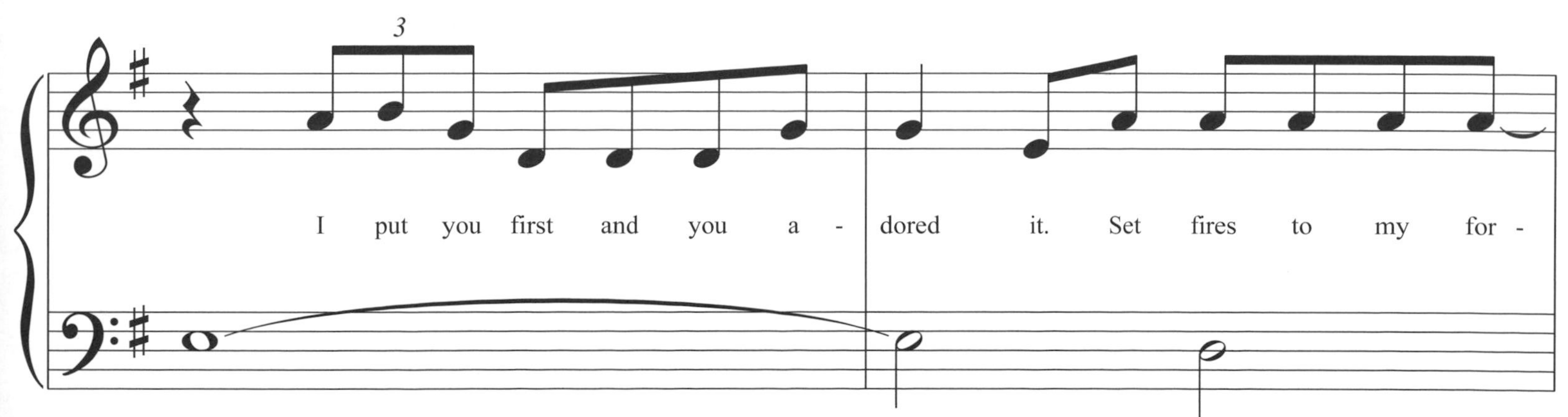

3
I put you first and you a - dored it. Set fires to my for -

- est, and you let it burn. Sang off - key in my cho -

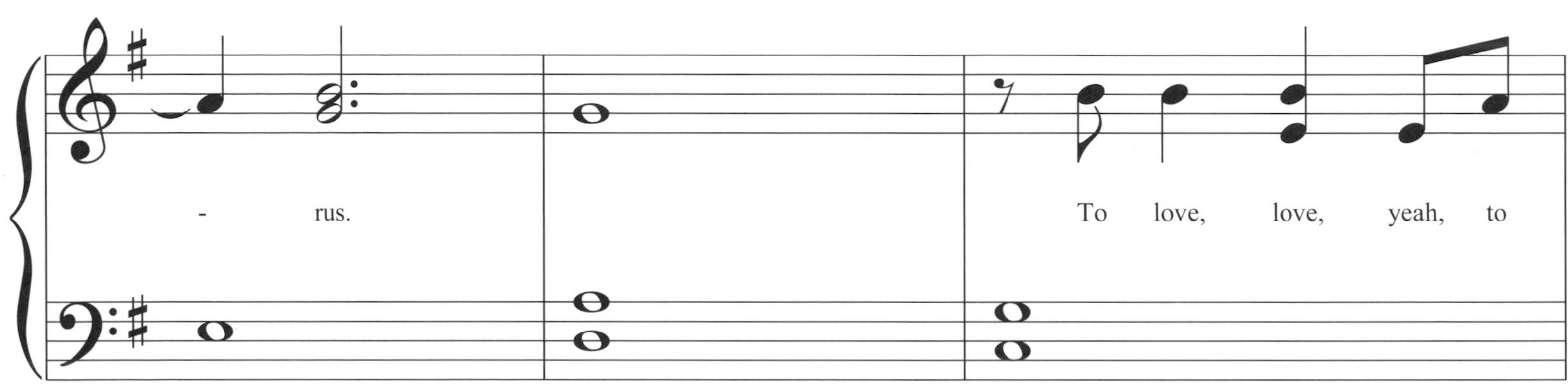
- rus. To love, love, yeah, to

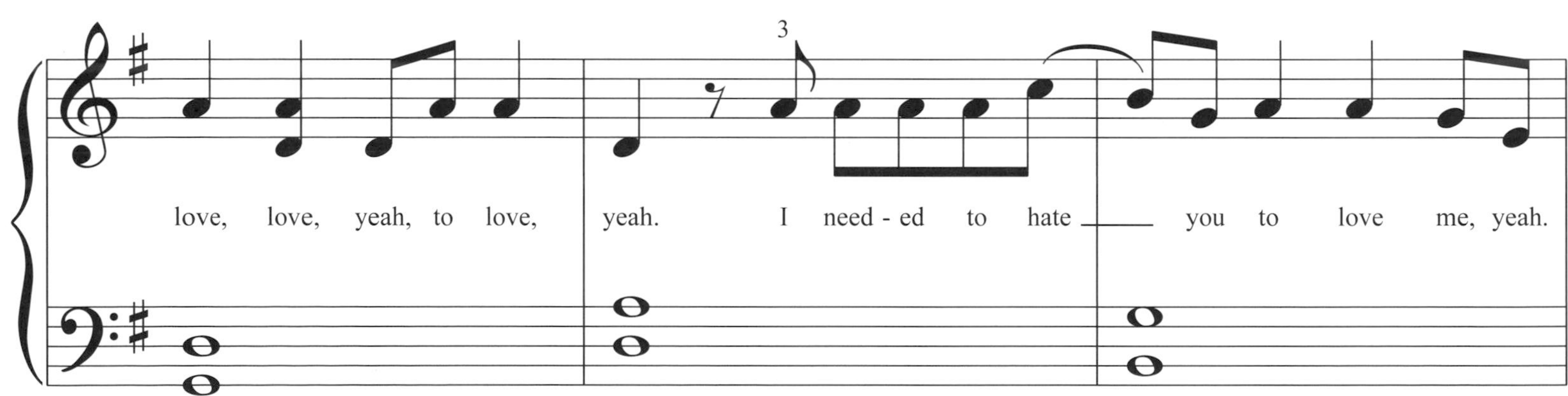
3
love, love, yeah, to love, yeah. I need - ed to hate you to love me, yeah.

To love, love, yeah, to love, love, yeah, to love, yeah. I need - ed to lose

you to love me.
To love, love, yeah, to love, love, yeah, to love,

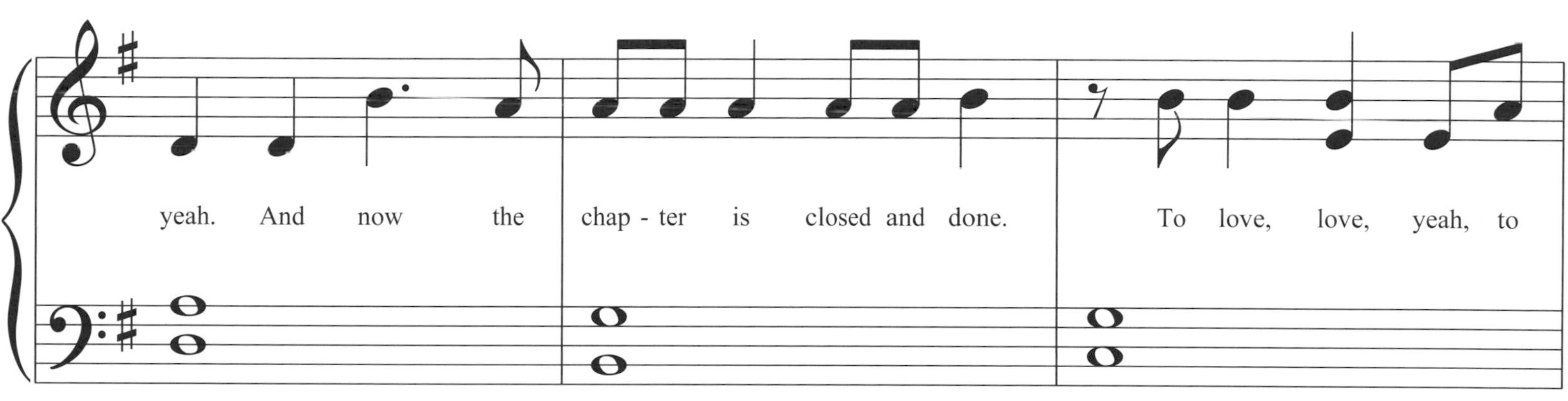
yeah. And now the chap - ter is closed and done.
To love, love, yeah, to

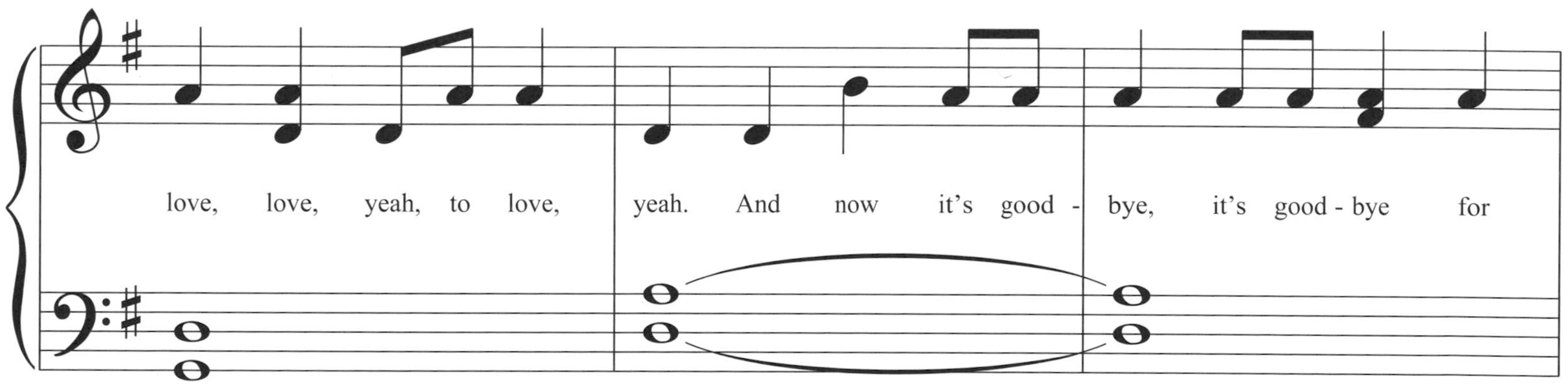
love, love, yeah, to love,
yeah. And now it's good - bye, it's good - bye for

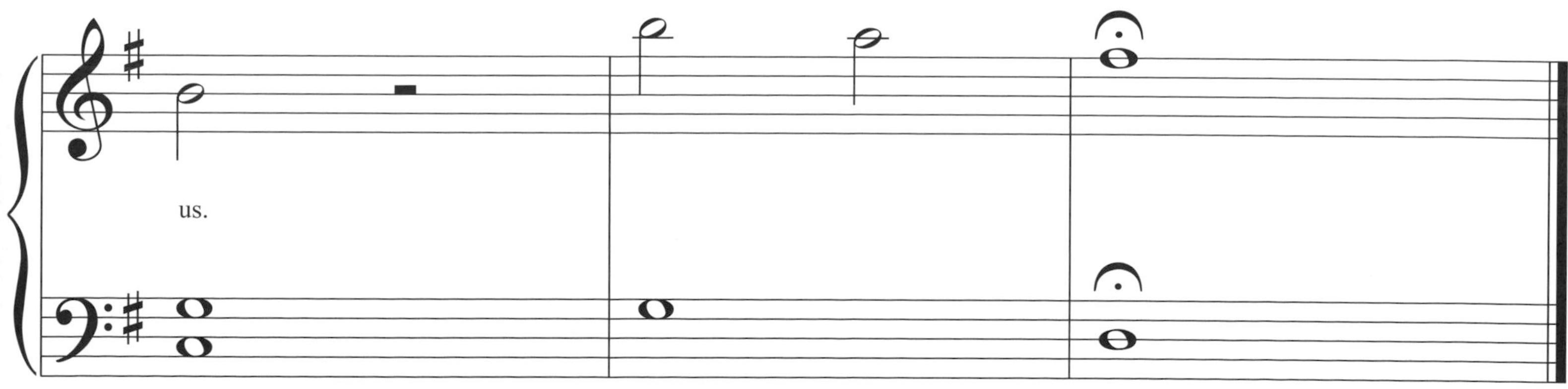
us.

LOVER

Words and Music by
TAYLOR SWIFT

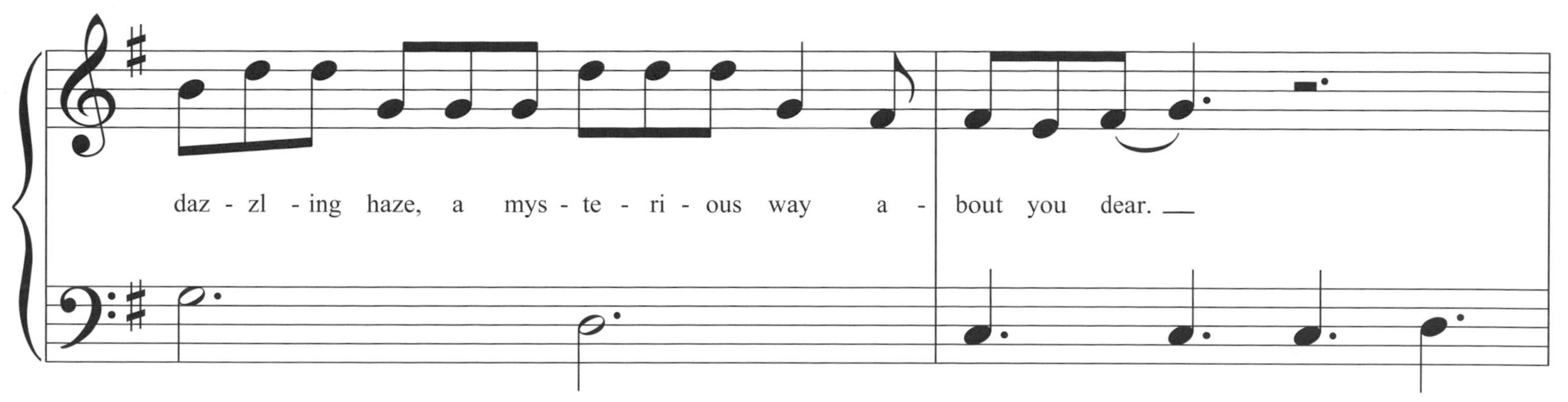
daz - zl - ing haze, a mys - te - ri - ous way a - bout you dear. ___

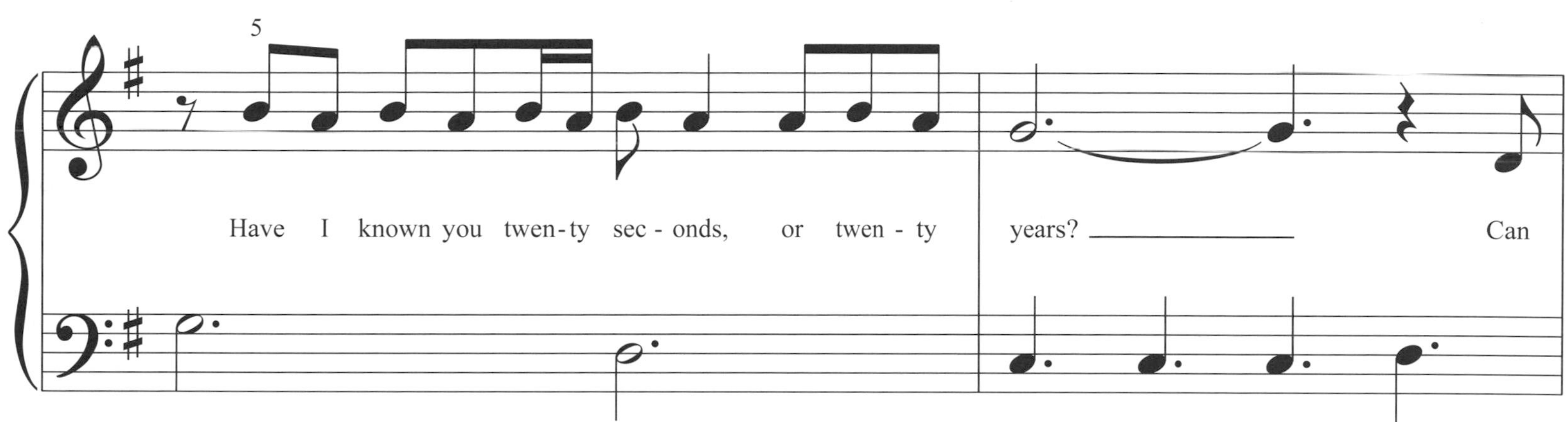
5
Have I known you twen-ty sec - onds, or twen - ty years? ___ Can

I go where you go? ___ Can we al - ways be this

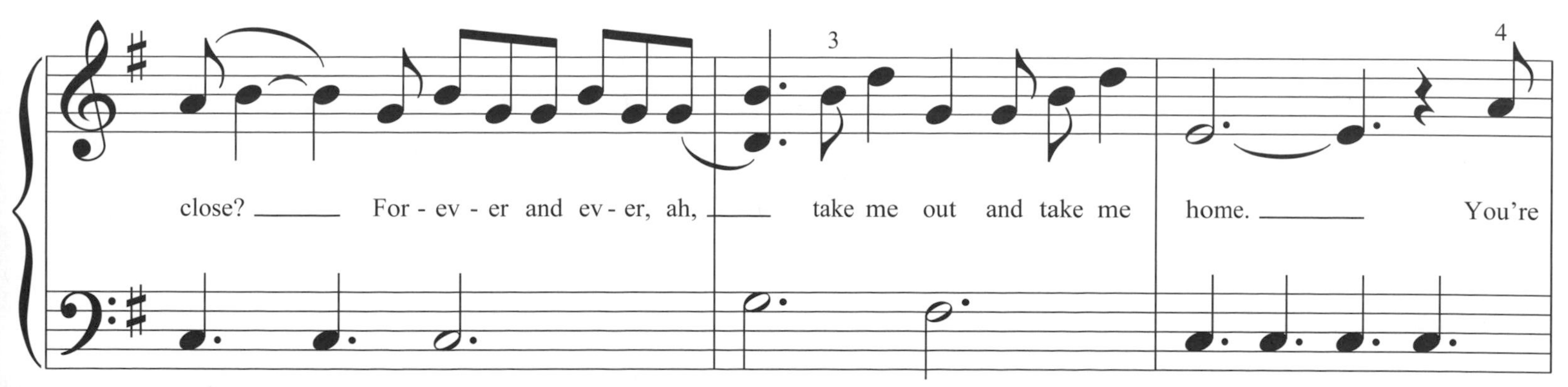
3
4
close? ___ For - ev - er and ev - er, ah, ___ take me out and take me home. ___ You're

To Coda
my, my, my, my lov - er.
1
We could let our friends crash in the
liv - ing room.
This is our place; we make the call.
I'm
high - ly sus - pi - cious that ev - 'ry - one who sees you
4
wants you.
I've

D.S. al Coda

loved you three sum - mers now, hon - ey, but I want 'em
all. Can

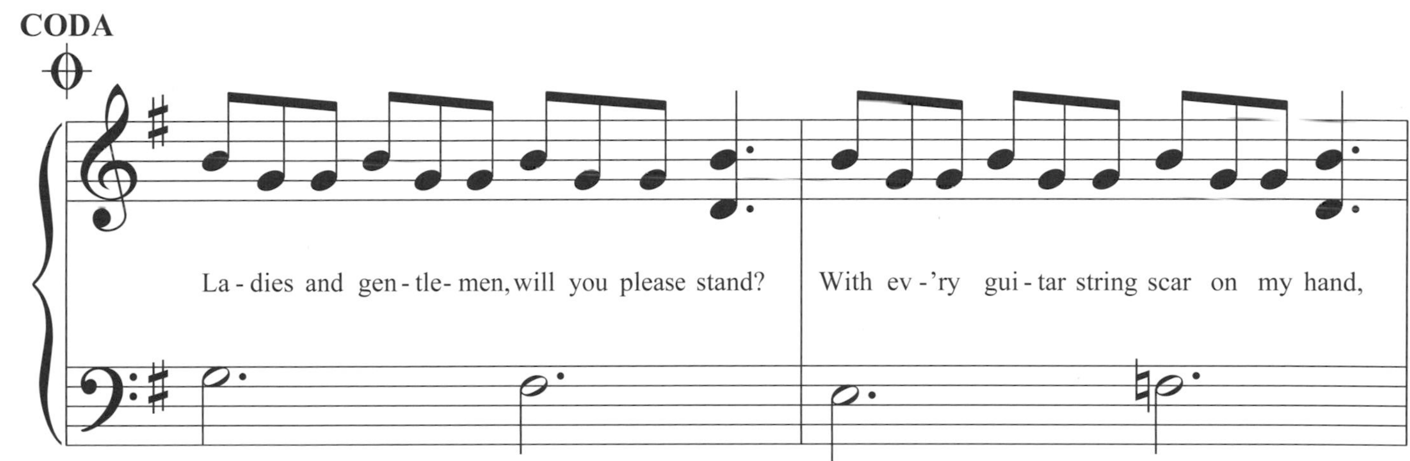
CODA
La - dies and gen - tle - men, will you please stand?
With ev - 'ry gui - tar string scar on my hand,

3
4
I take this mag - net - ic force of a man to be
my lov - er.

My heart's been bor - rowed and yours has been blue.
All's well that ends well, to end up with you.

Swear to be o - ver - dra - mat - ic and true to my lov - er. And
4

1
you'll save all your dirt - i - est jokes for me. And at ev - 'ry

ta - ble I'll save you a seat, lov - er. Can

I go where you go? Can we al - ways be this

4
close? For - ev - er and ev - er, ah, take me out and take me home. You're

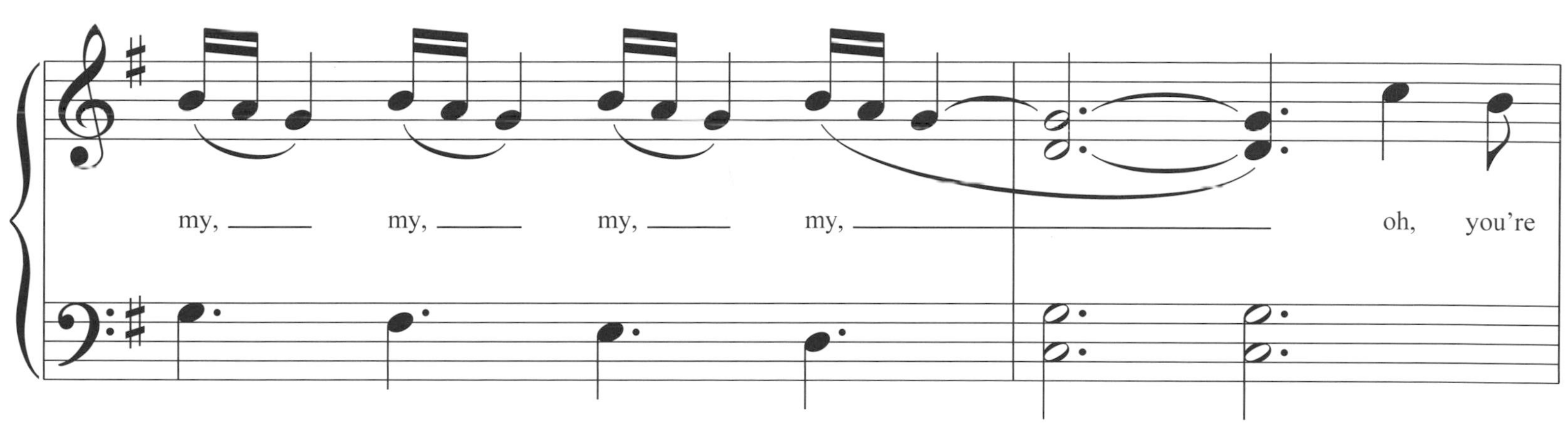
my, my, my, my, oh, you're

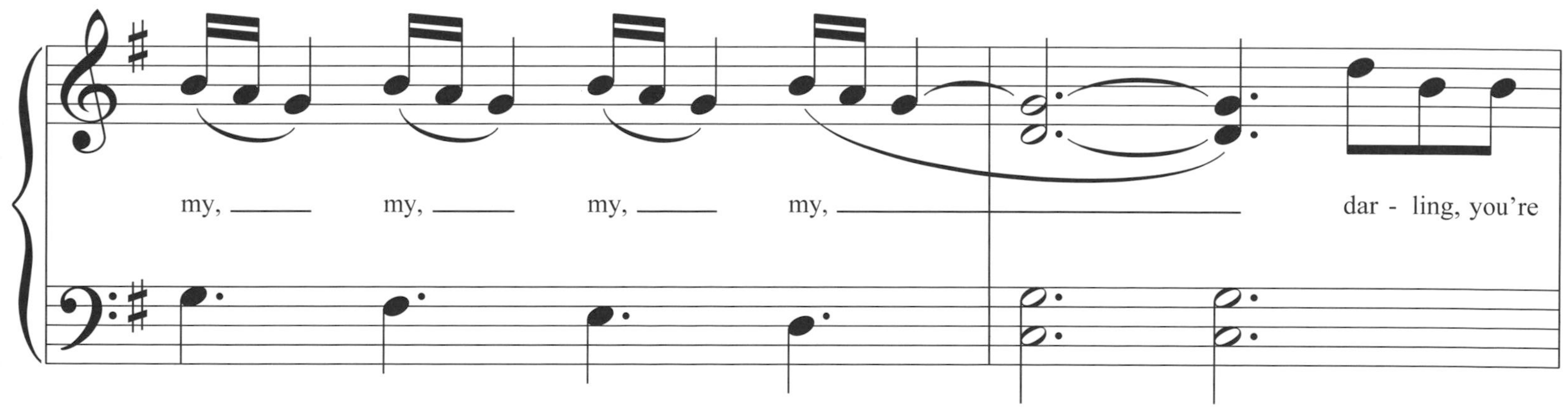
my, my, my, my, dar - ling, you're

my, my, my, my, lov - er.

MEMORIES

Words and Music by ADAM LEVINE,
JONATHAN BELLION, JORDAN JOHNSON,
JACOB HINDLIN, STEFAN JOHNSON,
MICHAEL POLLACK and VINCENT FORD

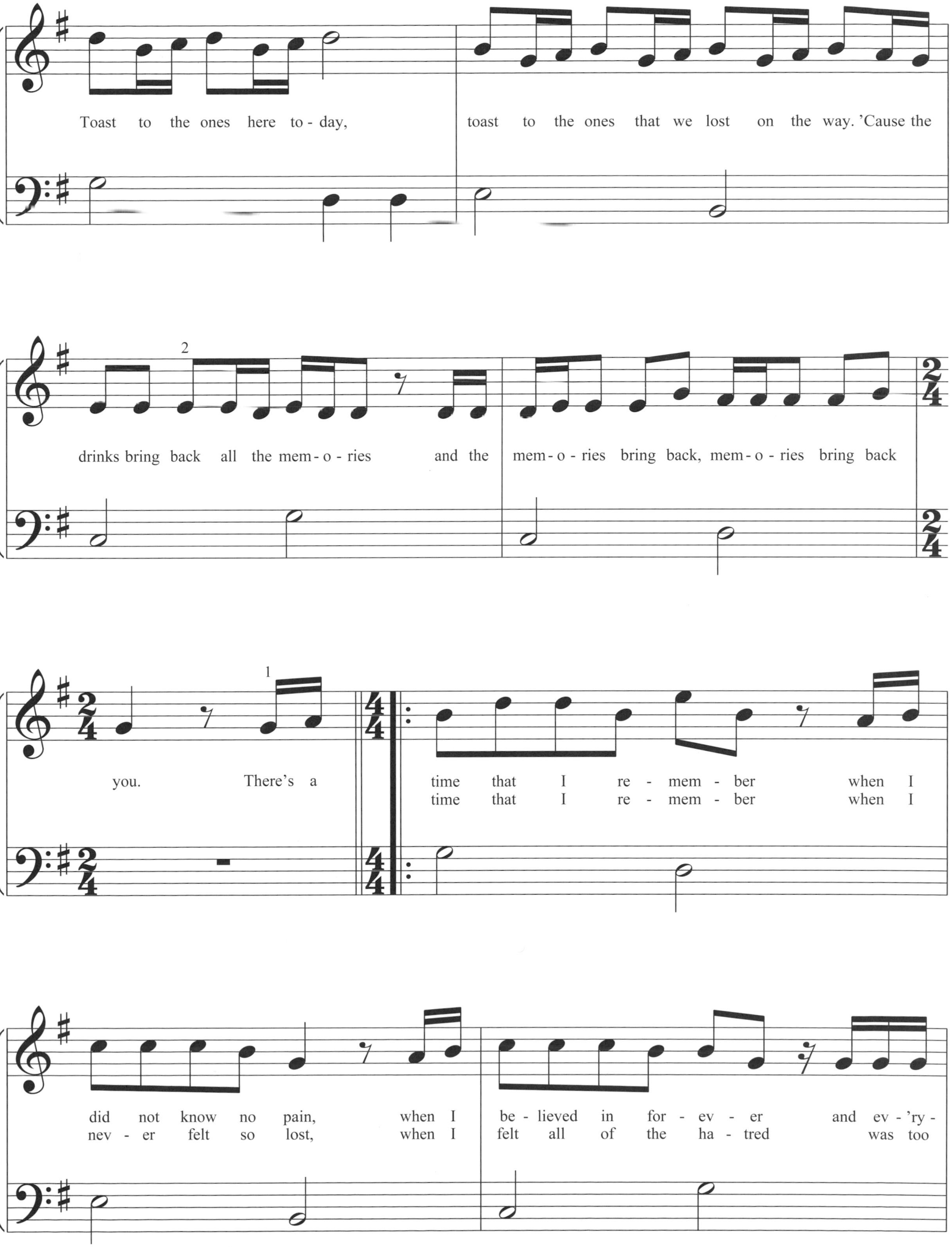

Toast to the ones here to - day, toast to the ones that we lost on the way. 'Cause the

2

drinks bring back all the mem - o - ries and the mem - o - ries bring back, mem - o - ries bring back

1

you. There's a time that I re - mem - ber when I
time that I re - mem - ber when I

thing would stay the same. Now my heart feel like De - cem - ber when some -
pow - er - ful to stop. Now my heart feel like an em - ber and it's
bod - y say your name, 'cause I can't reach out to call you, but I
light - ing up the dark, I'll car - ry these torch - es for you that you
know I will one day, yeah.
know I'll nev - er drop, yeah.
3
Ev - 'ry - bod - y hurts some - times,
ev - 'ry - bod - y hurts some - day, ay.
But ev - 'ry - thing gon' be al - right.

Go and raise a glass and say, ay. Here's to the ones that we got,
cheers to the wish you were here, but you're not. 'Cause the drinks bring back all the mem-o-ries of
ev-'ry-thing we've been through. Toast to the ones here to-day,
toast to the ones that we lost on the way. 'Cause the drinks bring back all the mem-o-ries and the

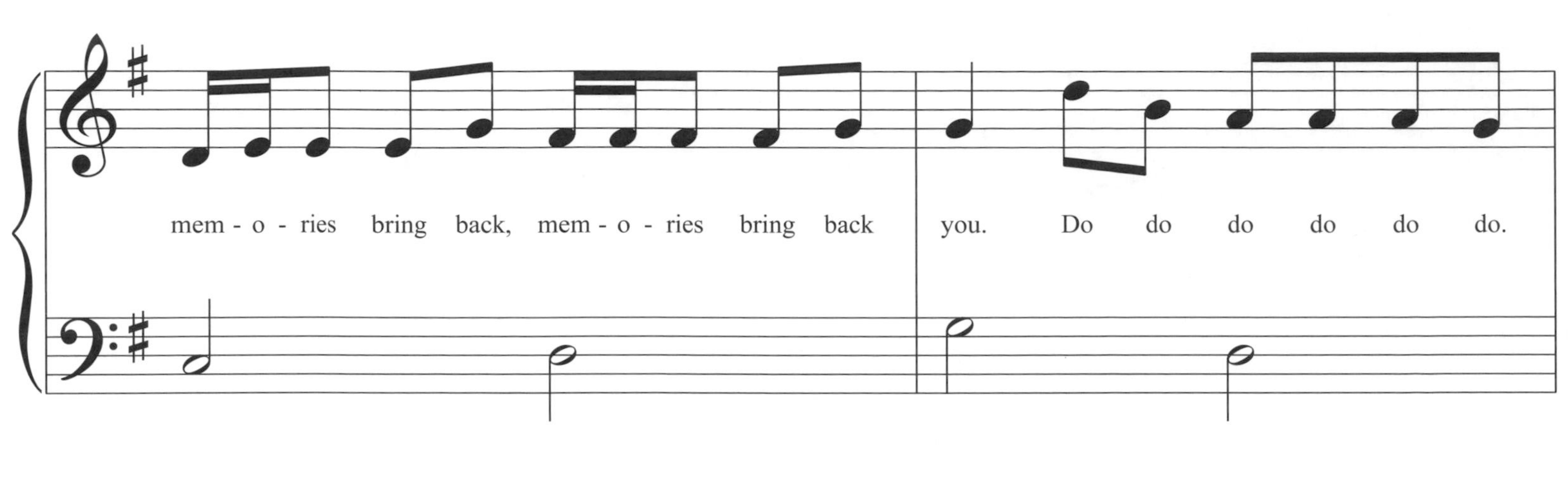
mem - o - ries bring back, mem - o - ries bring back
you. Do do do do do do.

Do do do do do do do do.
Do do do do do do do.

1.
1 2 1
Mem - o - ries bring back, mem - o - ries bring back
you. There's a

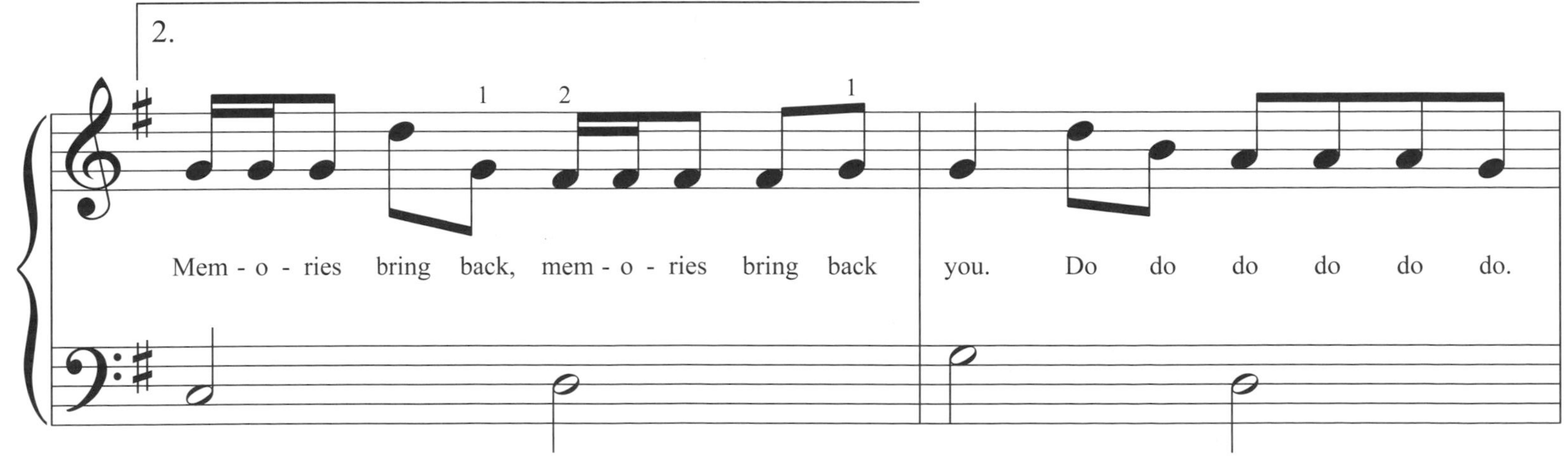
2.
1 2 1
Mem - o - ries bring back, mem - o - ries bring back
you. Do do do do do do.

Do do do do do do do do.
Do do do do do do do.

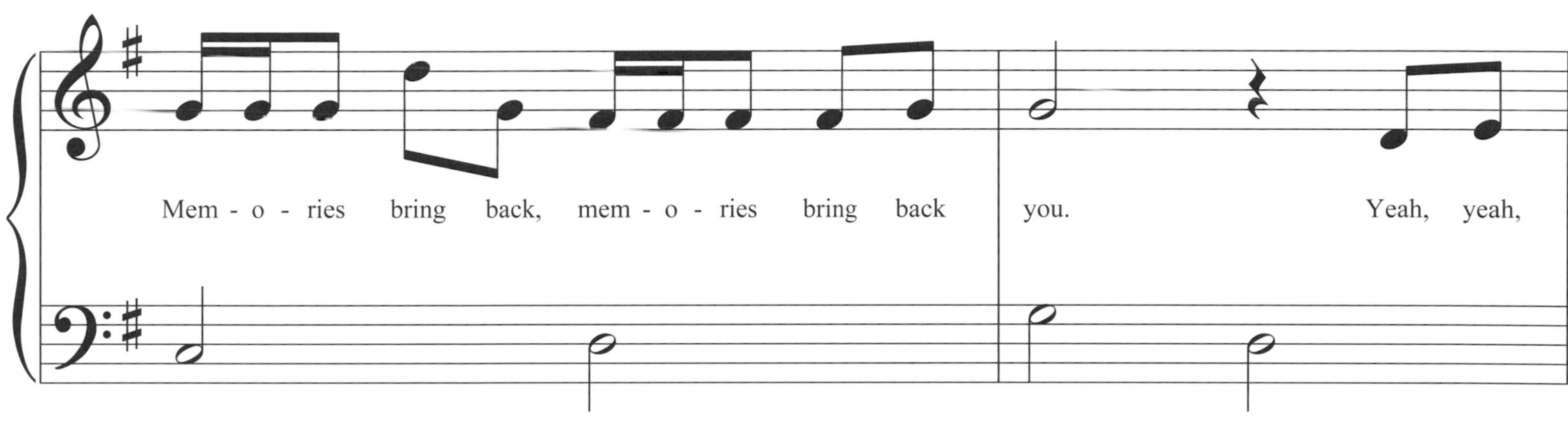
Mem - o - ries bring back, mem - o - ries bring back you.
Yeah, yeah,

3
yeah.
Yeah, yeah,
yeah, yeah, doh, doh.

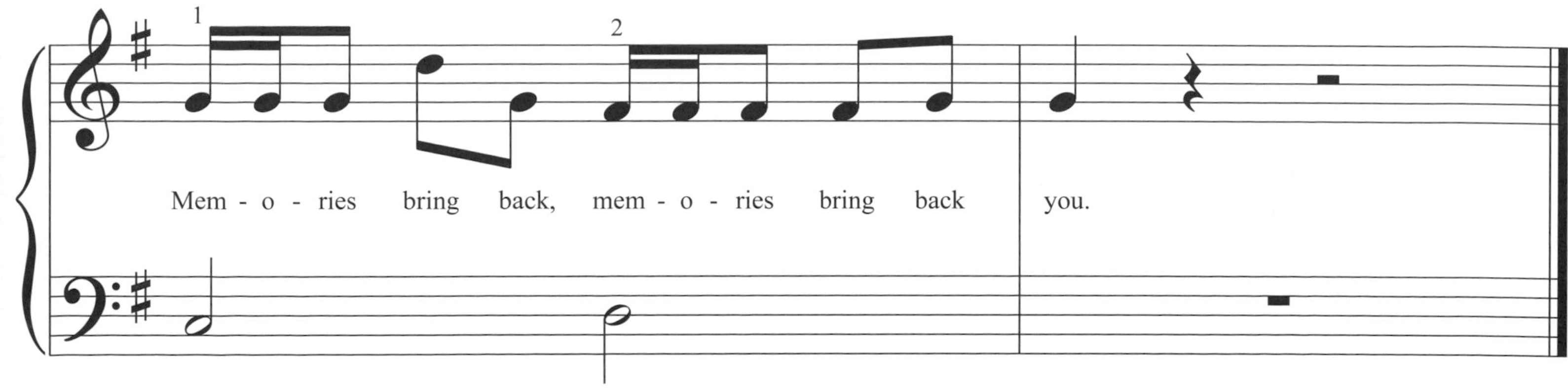
1
2
Mem - o - ries bring back, mem - o - ries bring back you.

10,000 HOURS

Words and Music by DAN SMYERS,
JORDAN REYNOLDS, SHAY MOONEY,
JUSTIN BIEBER, JASON BOYD
and JESSIE JO DILLON

3 2 1
close your eyes, tell me, what are you dream-ing? Ev-'ry-thing, I wan-na know it

1 3
all, mmm. I'd spend ten thou-sand ho - urs and
3

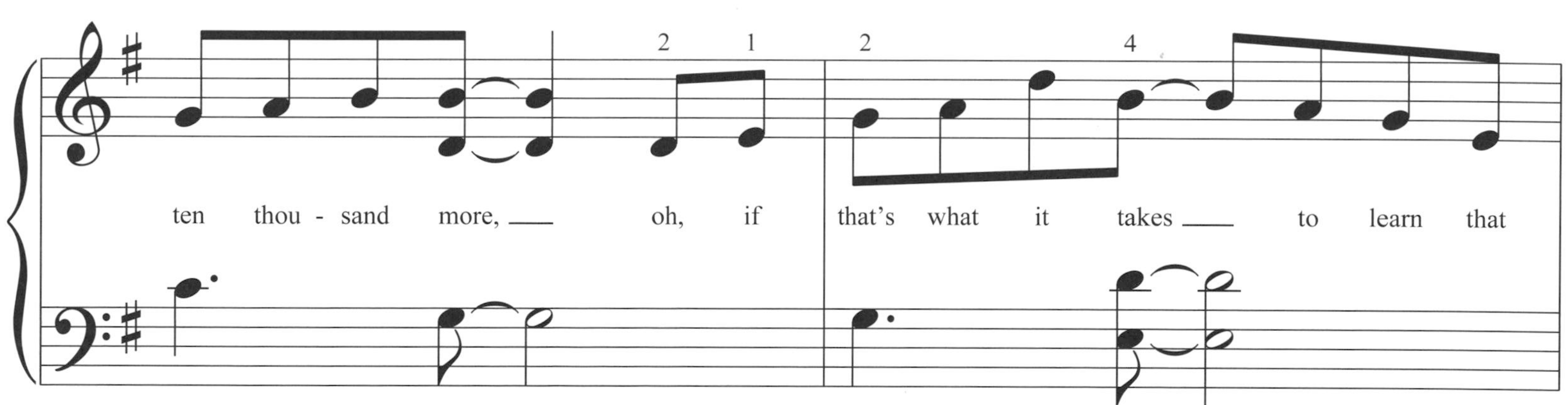
2 1 2 4
ten thou-sand more, oh, if that's what it takes to learn that

1 3
sweet heart of yours. And I might nev - er get there, but

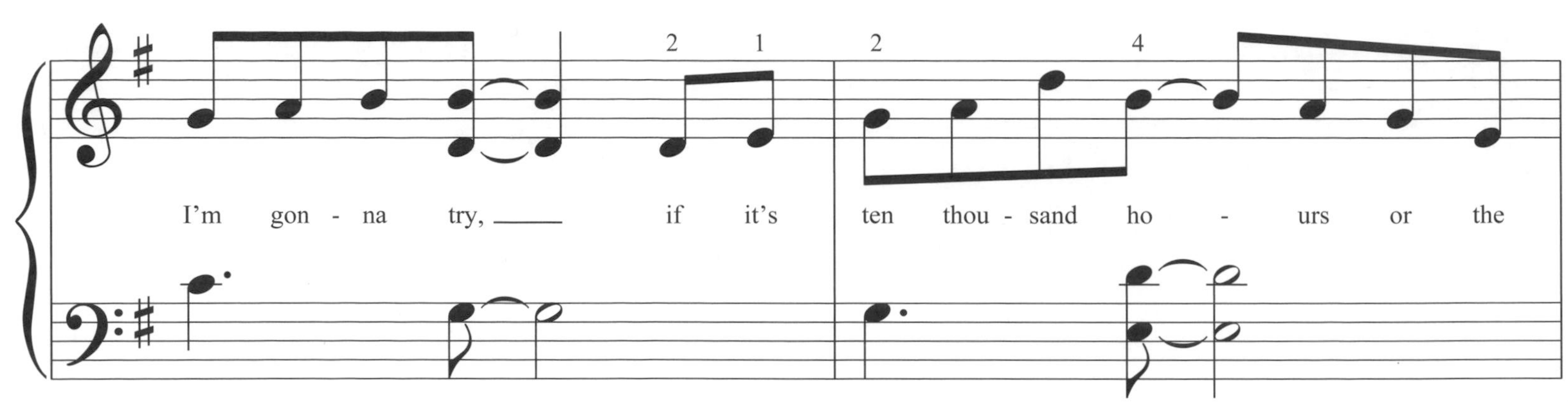
2 1 2 4
I'm gon - na try, if it's ten thou - sand ho - urs or the

1.
4
rest of my life. I'm gon - na love you. Ooh.

2.
To Coda
3
I'm gon - na love you.

1
3 3
Ooh, want the good and the bad, ev - 'ry - thing in be - tween.

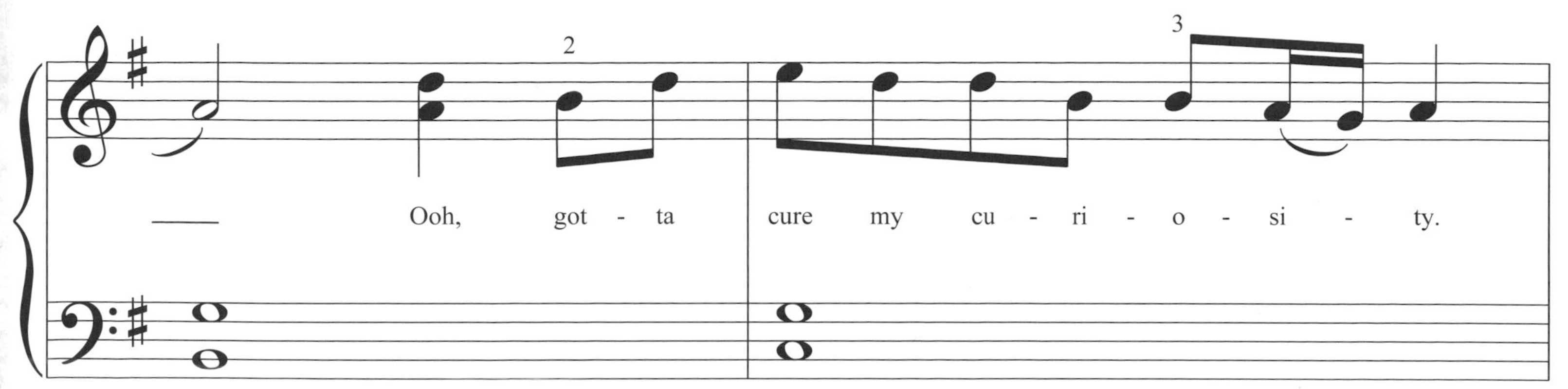

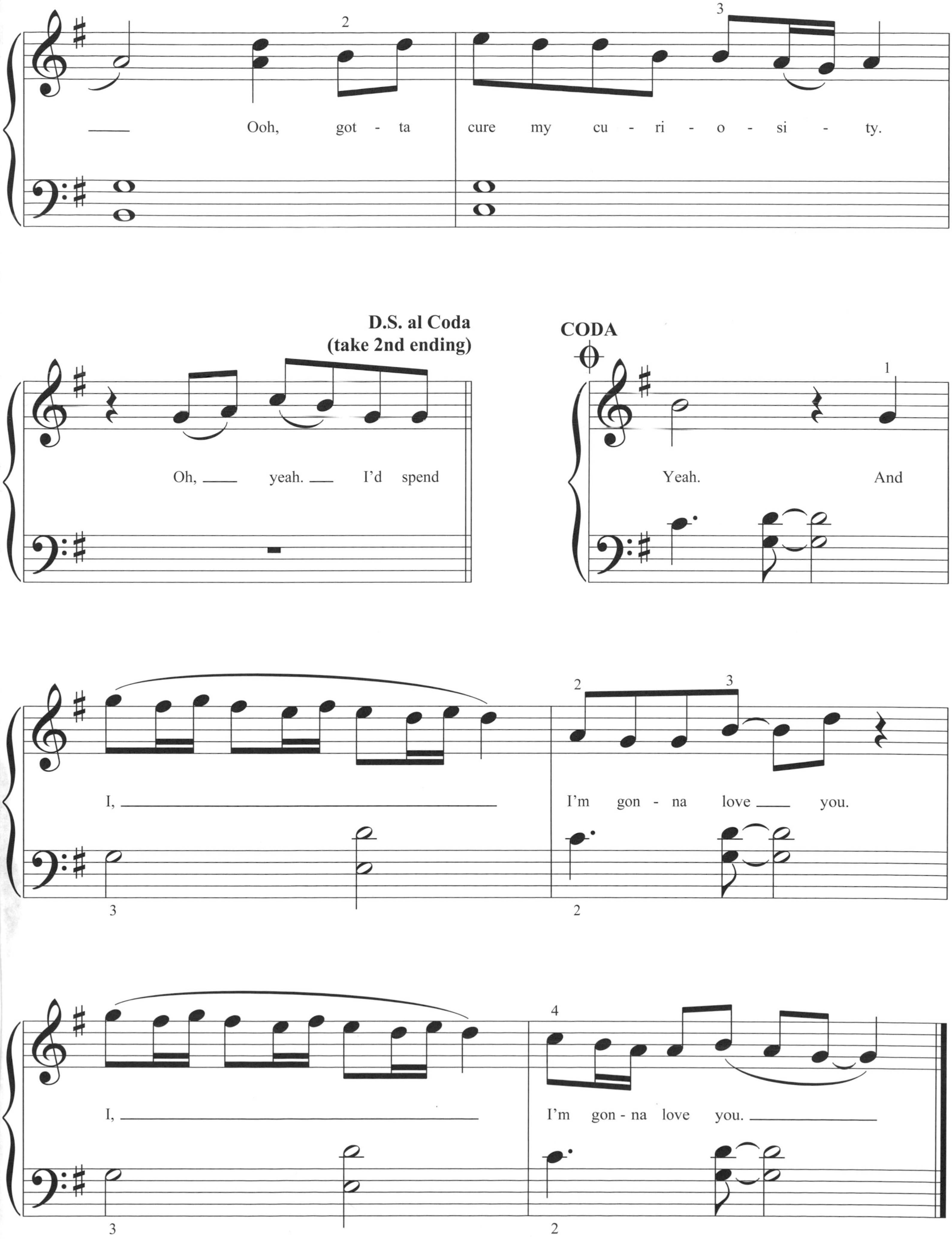

D.S. al Coda (take 2nd ending)

Oh, yeah. I'd spend

CODA

Yeah. And

I,

I'm gon - na love you.

I,

I'm gon - na love you.

Big Fun with Big-Note Piano Books!

These songbooks feature exciting easy arrangements for beginning piano students.

Best of Adele

Now even beginners can play their favorite Adele tunes! This book features big-note arrangements of 10 top songs: Chasing Pavements • Daydreamer • Hometown Glory • Lovesong • Make You Feel My Love • One and Only • Rolling in the Deep • Set Fire to the Rain • Someone like You • Turning Tables.
00308601 ....$14.99

Beatles' Best

27 classics for beginners to enjoy, including: Can't Buy Me Love • Eleanor Rigby • Hey Jude • Michelle • Here, There and Everywhere • When I'm Sixty-Four • Yesterday • and more.
00222561...$14.99

The Best Songs Ever

70 favorites, featuring: Body and Soul • Crazy • Edelweiss • Fly Me to the Moon • Georgia on My Mind • Imagine • The Lady Is a Tramp • Memory • A String of Pearls • Tears in Heaven • Unforgettable • You Are So Beautiful • and more.
00310425 ....$19.95

Children's Favorite Movie Songs

arranged by Phillip Keveren

16 favorites from films, including: The Bare Necessities • Beauty and the Beast • Can You Feel the Love Tonight • Do-Re-Mi • The Rainbow Connection • Tomorrow • Zip-A-Dee-Doo-Dah • and more.
00310838 ....$12.99

Classical Music's Greatest Hits

24 beloved classical pieces, including: Air on the G String • Ave Maria • By the Beautiful Blue Danube • Canon in D • Eine Kleine Nachtmusik • Für Elise • Ode to Joy • Romeo and Juliet • Waltz of the Flowers • more.
00310475 ....$12.99

Disney Big-Note Collection

Over 40 Disney favorites, including: Circle of Life • Colors of the Wind • Hakuna Matata • It's a Small World • Under the Sea • A Whole New World • Winnie the Pooh • Zip-A-Dee-Doo-Dah • and more.
00316056...$19.99

Essential Classical

22 simplified piano pieces from top composers, including: Ave Maria (Schubert) • Blue Danube Waltz (Strauss) • Für Elise (Beethoven) • Jesu, Joy of Man's Desiring (Bach) • Morning (Grieg) • Pomp and Circumstance (Elgar) • and many more.
00311205...$10.99

Favorite Children's Songs

arranged by Bill Boyd

29 easy arrangements of songs to play and sing with children: Peter Cottontail • I Whistle a Happy Tune • It's a Small World • On the Good Ship Lollipop • The Rainbow Connection • and more!
00240251...$12.99

Frozen

9 songs from this hit Disney film, plus full-color illustrations from the movie. Songs include the standout single "Let It Go", plus: Do You Want to Build a Snowman? • For the First Time in Forever • Reindeer(s) Are Better Than People • and more.
00126105 ....$12.99

Happy Birthday to You and Other Great Songs for Big-Note Piano

16 essential favorites, including: Chitty Chitty Bang Bang • Good Night • Happy Birthday to You • Heart and Soul • Over the Rainbow • Sing • This Land Is Your Land • and more.
00119636 ....$9.99

Elton John – Greatest Hits

20 of his biggest hits, including: Bennie and the Jets • Candle in the Wind • Crocodile Rock • Rocket Man • Tiny Dancer • Your Song • and more.
00221832...$14.99

Les Misérables

14 favorites from the Broadway sensation arranged for beginning pianists. Titles include: At the End of the Day • Bring Him Home • Castle on a Cloud • I Dreamed a Dream • In My Life • On My Own • Who Am I? • and more.
00221812 ....$15.99

The Phantom of the Opera

9 songs from the Broadway spectacular, including: All I Ask of You • Angel of Music • Masquerade • The Music of the Night • The Phantom of the Opera • The Point of No Return • Prima Donna • Think of Me • Wishing You Were Somehow Here Again.
00110006 ....$14.99

Pride & Prejudice

Music from the Motion Picture Soundtrack

12 piano pieces from the 2006 Oscar-nominated film: Another Dance • Darcy's Letter • Georgiana • Leaving Netherfield • Liz on Top of the World • Meryton Townhall • The Secret Life of Daydreams • Stars and Butterflies • and more.
00316125 ....$12.99

The Sound of Music

arranged by Phillip Keveren

9 favorites: Climb Ev'ry Mountain • Do-Re-Mi • Edelweiss • The Lonely Goatherd • Maria • My Favorite Things • Sixteen Going on Seventeen • So Long, Farewell • The Sound of Music.
00316057...$10.99

Best of Taylor Swift

A dozen top tunes from this crossover sensation: Fearless • Fifteen • Hey Stephen • Love Story • Our Song • Picture to Burn • Teardrops on My Guitar • White Horse • You Belong with Me • and more.
00307143 ....$12.99

Worship Favorites

20 powerful songs: Above All • Come, Now Is the Time to Worship • I Could Sing of Your Love Forever • More Precious Than Silver • Open the Eyes of My Heart • Shout to the Lord • and more.
00311207...$12.99

Complete song lists online at
www.halleonard.com

0719
060